info@kinfolk.com
www.kinfolk.com

*Kinfolk Magazine*
328 NE Failing Street
Portland, Oregon 97212
Telephone: 503-946-8400

Printed in Canada

Publication Design by Amanda Jane Jones
Cover Photograph by Maia Flore

# KINFOLK

**NATHAN WILLIAMS**
EDITOR IN CHIEF & CREATIVE DIRECTOR

**GEORGIA FRANCES KING**
EDITOR

**GAIL O'HARA**
MANAGING EDITOR

**JENNIFER JAMES WRIGHT**
ART DIRECTOR

**AMANDA JANE JONES**
LEAD DESIGNER

**DOUG BISCHOFF**
BUSINESS OPERATIONS

**KATIE SEARLE-WILLIAMS**
BUSINESS MANAGER

**PAIGE BISCHOFF**
ACCOUNTS PAYABLE & RECEIVABLE

**JOANNA HAN**
DEPUTY EDITOR

**JULIE POINTER**
COMMUNITY DIRECTOR

**JESSICA GRAY**
ASSISTANT COMMUNITY MANAGER

**NATHAN TICKNOR**
SERVICE MANAGER

**ERIC DAVIS**
WEB ADMINISTRATOR

**JORDAN HERNANDEZ**
EDITORIAL ASSISTANT

**HANNA PETTERSEN**
EDITORIAL ASSISTANT

**MARÍA DEL MAR SACASA**
RECIPE EDITOR

**KELSEY B. SNELL**
PROOFREADER

---

**SUBSCRIPTIONS**

*Kinfolk* is published four times a year.
To subscribe, visit *www.kinfolk.com/shop*
or email us at *subscribe@kinfolk.com*

**CONTACT US**

If you have questions or comments,
write to us at *info@kinfolk.com*

**WWW.KINFOLK.COM**

# WELCOME

*"We shape our dwellings, and afterwards our dwellings shape us"*
—Winston Churchill

Our concept of home grows and changes as the years and rent payments pass. When we were children, it was expressed through pillow forts, dollhouses and any place with a warm bed and a familiar face. Now we know there are as many types of residences as there are planks in picket fences. In this spring edition of *Kinfolk*—the Home Issue—we explore the notions of them all, from one-bedroom love shacks to sprawling family bungalows.

Lone rangers will find a decadent three-course meal designed for a single table setting, house guests are offered tips to guarantee repeat invitations and communal dwellers are given a guide to the notorious shared fridge. There are tips from creative types who work from home (and actually get things done), essays on buildings that live and breathe and a house sitter's reflection on what she can discern about you from the contents of your pantry.

We seek guidance from those who know their way around other people's abodes, such as the British design deity Sir Terence Conran and a bunch of award-winning Danish designers. Three London chefs invite us into their kitchens, and the former editor of the domestic bible *House & Garden* writes us an opening essay about what she's learned from decades of pondering about the meaning of home.

You may have noticed we've gained a little weight: That's because we've gone up a belt notch, adding an extra 32 pages at the back of this issue to invite you behind the front doors of homes around the world. Featuring stone-walled villas in Spain to flower-filled apartments in Indonesia, the Home Issue contains a diverse mix of living spaces that represent alternative ways of nesting.

What we've learned is that it doesn't matter how you decorate your mantel, the hue of white on your walls or the number of earthenware mugs in your kitchen. Home is what you make it, and we'd like to celebrate the well-made. Welcome.

NATHAN WILLIAMS AND GEORGIA FRANCES KING

ROMY ASH
*Writer*
*Melbourne, Australia*

NABIL SABIO AZADI
*Writer*
*Brisbane, Australia*

NEIL BEDFORD
*Photographer*
*London, United Kingdom*

MÒNICA BEDMAR
*Photographer*
*Galicia, Spain*

RYAN BENYI
*Photographer*
*Queens, New York*

NILS BERNSTEIN
*Writer*
*New York, New York*

EBONY BIZYS
*Writer*
*Tokyo, Japan*

JONAS BJERRE-POULSEN
*Photographer*
*Copenhagen, Denmark*

CATHLEEN BOYDRON
*Writer*
*Paris, France*

LUISA BRIMBLE
*Photographer*
*Sydney, Australia*

DOMINIQUE BROWNING
*Writer*
*New York, New York*

SARAH BURWASH
*Illustrator*
*Nova Scotia, Canada*

LIZ CLAYTON
*Writer*
*Brooklyn, New York*

KATRIN COETZER
*Illustrator*
*Cape Town, South Africa*

DAVID COGGINS
*Writer*
*New York, New York*

KIRSTY DAVEY
*Photographer*
*Jan Juc, Australia*

CARLY DIAZ
*Writer*
*Portland, Oregon*

TRAVIS ELBOROUGH
*Writer*
*London, United Kingdom*

PHILIP FICKS
*Photographer*
*Brooklyn, New York*

JAMES FITZGERALD III
*Photographer*
*Portland, Oregon*

PARKER FITZGERALD
*Photographer*
*Portland, Oregon*

MAIA FLORE
*Photographer*
*Paris, France*

ALICE GAO
*Photographer*
*New York, New York*

GENTL & HYERS
*Photographers*
*New York, New York*

SKYE GYNGELL
*Writer*
*London, United Kingdom*

HIDEAKI HAMADA
*Photographer*
*Osaka, Japan*

FERGUS HENDERSON
*Writer*
*London, United Kingdom*

INDIA HOBSON
*Photographer*
*Sheffield, United Kingdom*

DITTE ISAGER
*Photographer*
*Copenhagen, Denmark*

OLIVIA RAE JAMES
*Photographer*
*Charleston, South Carolina*

KATE S. JORDAN
*Prop Stylist*
*Pound Ridge, New York*

LINE T. KLEIN
*Photographer*
*Copenhagen, Denmark*

FLORENCE KNIGHT
*Writer*
*London, United Kingdom*

KATHRIN KOSCHITZKI
*Photographer*
*Nuremberg, Germany*

HELEN MACINTYRE
*Set Designer*
*London, United Kingdom*

JOSUE MARTINEZ
*Writer*
*Bali, Indonesia*

ANNA MOLLER
*Photographer*
*Brooklyn, New York*

FRANCES PALMER
*Ceramist*
*Weston, Connecticut*

LEO PATRONE
*Photographer*
*Salt Lake City, Utah*

TEC PETAJA
*Photographer*
*Nashville, Tennessee*

NIKAELA MARIE PETERS
*Writer*
*Winnipeg, Canada*

CHRIS & SARAH RHOADS
*Photographers*
*Seattle, Washington*

TIM ROBISON
*Photographer*
*Asheville, North Carolina*

STEPHANIE ROSENBAUM
*Writer*
*San Francisco, California*

KATHERINE SACKS
*Writer*
*Berlin, Germany*

AMELIA SCHMIDT
*Writer*
*Melbourne, Australia*

NATHALIE SCHWER
*Stylist*
*Copenhagen, Denmark*

SAKIKO SETAKA
*Kinfolk Japan Assistant*
*Tokyo, Japan*

VICTORIA SMITH
*Writer*
*San Francisco, California*

KATIE STRATTON
*Painter*
*Dayton, Ohio*

STUDIO OINK
*Photographers*
*Wiesbaden, Germany*

VICKY TANZIL
*Photographer*
*Jakarta, Indonesia*

SIMON TAYLOR
*Photographer*
*Jan Juc, Australia*

DAVID WINWARD
*Writer*
*Salt Lake City, Utah*

# ONE

# TWO

# FEW

# A MANIFESTO FOR THE WELL-WORN HOME

*Dominique Browning has spent decades considering what
goes into building a well-worn home: the best kind there is.
Let fabric age, embrace the flaws and gather meaningful items,
and your home will start to feel loved and lived-in.*

The idea came to me when we were settling into our friend's living room, having just enjoyed a delectable meal. I was nestling into a pillow, which was exactly the right shape for a back aching after a day of gardening, when a shawl draped over the armchair slipped off, revealing a long tear in the upholstery.

"I know, but…" my friend said, catching my eye. "I haven't been able to bring myself to re-cover it. I've loved that fabric for years."

I knew exactly what she meant: Just that morning I'd slipped an old cozy over a steaming teapot and its silk cover split as though it was tissue paper. But I could never throw it away—it was a gift from a beloved friend 35 years ago. It's as much a part of my home as my front door.

I've been thinking about houses, and what makes them work, for decades now. Over the years I've come to appreciate the profound beauty in all that's well-worn. The gentle accumulation of the things that grace our rooms and the memories they hold are what turn a house into a home.

All of our busyness with homemaking—the finding of a nest, the feathering of it—should be part of the larger journey of living, not simply an end in itself. We get so turned around with anxiety about what goes with what and what goes where. I've certainly been in the grip of that, though I've finally learned some tricks: Take cues about palette from the natural world around you and cues about seating arrangements from watching the way your friends gather. But interior design is so much simpler and yet so much deeper—or, at least, the best of it is. Here are some thoughts on how to create that well-worn home.

**LIVE WITH FEWER THINGS THAT HAVE GREATER MEANING** I would rather have one beautiful wheel-thrown bowl than a set of five from a factory. I'd rather spend too much on something special than spend just a little bit on mediocre things. Decide to use the best of what you have, often. Every day is a special occasion.

**STRIVE FOR IMPERFECTION** Accept blemishes and wrinkles—live with materials that age, rather than degrade. After having succumbed too often to their ways, I'm now wary of modern materials that age poorly. What's more beautiful than a heavy wooden cutting board etched with the marks of countless meals? What's more revealing than the scars around keyholes from trembling hands unlocking a desk drawer to hide love letters? What's more charming than the cigarette burns in the top of an old pub table, testifying to years of intense arguments and affairs?

**THE HANDMADE GLOWS WITH A HUMAN TOUCH** There's nothing more appealing than the feel of the crafter's hand. Every morning when I drink my tea from a cup made by a friend, its two handles resting on porcelain hips, I am comforted. The slight chip in the lip that I've contributed reminds me to slow down when I handle what's precious.

**DON'T BE AFRAID TO FALL IN LOVE** If something—a shape, a color, a touch—turns your head, then go for it. If you're undecided, walk away. Objects have an afterimage that burns into your soul. If it was meant to be in your life, then you'll return and take it home. But nothing waits forever. So follow your instincts.

**BE INTIMATE** Never keep your hands to yourself around the house. When was the last time you ran a palm over the surface of your old kitchen table and felt the ripples of hand-planed wood? Home is a place to peel back the layers, a place in which we feel safe enough to turn things upside down and inside out.

**HONOR THE PASSAGE OF TIME** Everything has a beginning, a start in life. Everything was once new. Every yard of fabric comes fresh and wet off the dyer's table. Every board leaves the sawmill gleaming. That's just the beginning of the history. Living in our houses is about letting our rooms mellow, letting our fabrics fade and soften, letting our tables scuff and scar, letting our rooms capture our stories. Those are *our* traces; they're born of our accidents and intentions.

**HANG ON FOR DEAR LIFE** Our things, and even our homes, seem to be more disposable than ever. We feel trapped in a cycle of using and tossing. We don't repair: We replace. We're bombarded with a new cultural imperative, reinforced by countless advertising messages to renew and refresh our furniture, our fashions and our faces. It's time to resist. We're in for a cultural—and domestic—reset.

*Dominique Browning is the senior director of Moms Clean Air Force. She writes for* The New York Times *and was the editor in chief of* House & Garden *for more than a decade.*

# ONE

ENTERTAINING FOR ONE

○

# LIVING FOR ONE: FLYING SOLO

WORDS BY VICTORIA SMITH & PHOTOGRAPH BY RYAN BENYI
SCULPTURE BY FRANCES PALMER

*Sometimes nests are built for one. A lot more life can be crammed into a home when the silverware drawer and linen closet aren't overflowing. After living solitary for decades, one writer reflects on the happiness it has brought.*

Living alone allows for freedoms you might never discover if there were other people around. Some of these little luxuries include listening to a scratchy Joni Mitchell vinyl record looping all weekend long, sleeping with nothing but two immensely fluffy duvets (no matter the season) and the utter glee these kinds of simple indulgences bring you and only you.

I often think the longer I live alone, the more eccentric I become. And I am, without a doubt, a creature of quirky habits. At home I wear my comfiest PJs and socks, but not unattractive ones—appearance is important, even when alone. I only wear white socks around the house, never black, as I find dark socks make you look like a lonely businessman wandering around a dingy hotel room (one of the odd things I contemplate with too much time on my own). I've also fallen into contented rhythms: I start with foggy early morning walks with my dog Lucy, coffee at the place that knows my name and order by heart, then back on home to work, again alone.

During my afternoons typing away, NPR acts as my company, allowing me to discover what's going on outside of my self-imposed cocoon. When the news gets too dark, I ditch it for an eclectic radio station played out of a community college basement somewhere in Santa Monica and sing along. I don't sing well, but it doesn't matter: It's another one of the perks and perils of living on your own.

My home has become a companion of sorts. It's filled with collections that evoke the stuff of joyful memories, making it a place I really like to be. A delightful thing about living alone is that I can put things wherever I want: I have a tendency to keep a certain order here, nothing out of place, everything just so. More often than not I have fresh flowers and most nights I burn candles. Hours are spent idly puttering around my little cottage and I've come to savor those rather uneventful moments, such as curating a photo exhibit on my fridge that few will ever view. Some nights I make my favorite recipes, or on others I'll simply nuke a baked potato and eat it standing up. Occasionally, when we're naughty, Lucy and I eat dinner in bed. No one minds when spaghetti sauce splashes the sheets.

I'm not immune to the idea of sharing my home with another human, but most days I'm pretty content. Have I grown too comfortable and rooted in my ways? Perhaps, which is not to say I wouldn't one day allow the right fellow in—one who finds my eccentricities adorable, or at least tolerable. For now, I savor these solo days like someone whose library book is overdue but hasn't quite finished the last chapter. There are still a few more pages to go. ○

*Victoria Smith is a photographer, writer and creative director of* SF Girl by Bay, *a website based in San Francisco, and one of the founders of Makeshift Society, a creative coworking space.*

# THE INTERNATIONAL SYMBOL OF HOME

WORDS BY KATHERINE SACKS & PHOTOGRAPH BY PARKER FITZGERALD

*After coming through the door, people around the world put
their best feet forward by stepping into their slippers. As one expat
has discovered, wearing them around the house not only keeps
your toes snug but also makes for a happier home.*

When we moved to Berlin last year, we were warned that some realtors are cautious about renting to foreigners. This isn't some outlandish example of expat-phobia but instead a recognition of the care of a home. In Germany, the house is a sacred space with many specific customs, and if dwellers haven't been raised to learn these cultural norms then they can unintentionally create problems.

Our first Berlin apartment came by way of a friend who happily explained many of these customs: Open the windows for a few minutes when arriving home to let in a *frischluft* (a stream of fresh air); painstakingly sort the plastic, paper, compost and garbage into their specific bins; and most importantly, take your boots off inside and replace them with slippers.

The idea of a shoeless house was a bit off-putting at first: Wearing shoes indoors can provide that necessary feeling of being ready to conquer the day, whereas slippers prepare you to tuck into a good book on the couch. But unlike the general custom in the US (and in many other Western countries), most Germans remove them and slip on *hausschuhe,* which literally translates to "house shoes." These beautifully handcrafted felted slippers are classically backless, some have rubber bottoms, but all are reserved for indoor use only.

Many other cultures practice the removal of footwear. Traditional Asian homes often have a small step at the entrance, providing an actual physical motion that signifies entrance into a private space. Some Japanese rental agreements even require that they'll not be worn in the home. Such cultures believe that taking off your shoes allows you to physically and mentally leave the dirt of the world outside.

As time passed, I began to notice something I hadn't in our previous houses: the small signs of the outdoors being tracked inside when I left my sneakers on. The more familiar we became with wearing our hausschuhe, the more we discovered that this modest change in our etiquette led to a greater quality of life, not only in cleanliness, but also in the comfort it provided.

In the past year, the simple act of removing our shoes has reshaped the consideration for our space. It has become a special tradition for us that feels almost ceremonious, in part because we're slowly feeling closer to our adopted German culture but also because of the quiet and peace it brings into our home. Unlike wearing slippers for comfort, we were actively taking care of our apartment in a way we hadn't before. When we eventually found our own to rent, we purchased a large cabinet and stocked it with several pairs of hausschuhe for visiting guests. Now the occasional sound of our shoes indoors feels out of place, and I'm quick to catch even the smallest amount of leaves or sand tracked into the foyer. It's a simple thought, but one that brings an extra touch of purity and warmth into the home. ○

*Katherine Sacks is an American journalist living in Berlin. A former pastry chef, she focuses on restaurant trends, travel writing and the people behind food. She also chronicles her cooking adventures on her website La Vita Cucinare.*

PHOTO ESSAY

# BECOMING YOUR HOME

*Sometimes we spend so much time cooped up at home that we're not just climbing the walls—we're becoming one with the woodwork. This photo essay takes a look at what happens when you and your surroundings begin to blend.*

PHOTOGRAPHS BY MAIA FLORE

# A GENTLEMAN'S GUIDE TO FENG SHUI

WORDS BY DAVID COGGINS & PHOTOGRAPH BY PARKER FITZGERALD

*There's no need to live in a black-leather bachelor pad or a frat house.*
*Our gentleman's guide to setting up a grown-up home*
*will help you leave all that stuff in the past.*

Men living on their own are rarely mistaken for interior designers. In fact, the cultural bar has been set relatively low thanks to such widely held associations as "the man cave." The assumption is that men, when left to their own devices, will revert to a premodern state, stop grooming themselves, have the television locked on the sports channel and subsist entirely on takeout. Here are a few simple things you can do to counter that assumption and prove you are a truly evolved modern man.

**TWO GOOD CHAIRS** Chairs facing each other invite conversation with a guest—it's the physical metaphor for friendship. They can be club chairs, they can be spare, they can be Danish. They can be new or old but they should be inviting, calling you across the room to come, sit down and share a bottle of wine. If space allows, please don't set them in front of the television. If your chair is comfortable but unsightly or beginning to come apart, just throw a piece of fabric over part of it—there's nothing wrong with that. Furniture should look used, like a corduroy coat with elbow patches.

**BOOKS** You can't have too many. I'm suspicious of any man who doesn't have the ambition to build a library. Your life should be full of anthologies of letters, definitive biographies, doomed poets, forgotten painters, Finnish country houses, Japanese textiles, old Sotheby's catalogs—there's a lot to page through. If you can afford it, start buying the catalogs of every good museum exhibition you see. After a few years, you'll be surprised how grateful you are to have a nice personal history of what you've seen.

**RUGS** Your wooden floors are shy. They don't want to be naked—they want to be covered. Get some nice rugs. It's not hard: Go to an estate sale or search eBay. There will be plenty to choose from and they won't be expensive. If you find one you're set on, get it, otherwise layer a few, layer 10, emulate a souk market. It's empowering.

**DOWNSIZE YOUR TV** Your house is a not an entertainment center, so you don't need a television the size of a large aquarium. Your life is better than TV: You travel, you date, you read novels. Enjoy some quality analog time, or even stare out the window—the original reality television.

**GOOD LIGHTS** Few things are less flattering than harsh overhead lights. Every restaurant you like has good lighting and your apartment should too. You could also get a few small side lamps and some old candlesticks—don't underestimate candlelight. It flatters rooms and, more importantly, faces.

**THE LONG VIEW** An apartment, like a wardrobe, isn't built in a day. Acquire things over time when you travel or luck into the perfect antique store. Improbable objects are a blessing: pheasant feathers, little plastic farm animals, old corkscrews or maybe an old lobster trap buoy. Don't worry; it will make sense one day. In the end you'll have an apartment that suits you, and that's a space worth aspiring to. ○

*David Coggins lives in a very full apartment in New York. His work has appeared in* Esquire, Interview *and* Art in America, *among other places.*

# NOTES FROM A HOUSE SITTER

WORDS BY STEPHANIE ROSENBAUM & PHOTOGRAPH BY TEC PETAJA

*What does your home say about you? A house sitter can tell from a five-minute snoop in your pantry, sprouting potatoes and all. One regular minder recalls some unexpected discoveries.*

Your house can't wait to tell its secrets to a stranger with a key. Friends of the household only see your home's most flattering angle: its curated, Instagram-ready, lavender-soap-and-fresh-coffee version of itself. An invited guest is expected to be politely, deliberately blind to the messier things, but your sitter stranger sees a different home: one imbued with mystery and intrigue, rife with hidden stories and a clandestine life.

Who would expect this tidy bungalow, owned by an engineer in his 60s, to have both a Tesla coil in the living room and an open-air shower in the backyard? He pointed them out with pride but left me to discover, a week after he'd left, that I'd also been cohabiting with a loaded pistol on the laundry room shelf, stashed casually between the Tide and a dozen bottles of cheap red.

In another place, the immaculate Danish-born owners requested I towel-dry their bathroom's vintage redwood surrounds after every shower. Yet they neglected to mention, until it was too late, that they'd exiled the household's sole toilet plunger to a locked shed in the backyard. Was it for aesthetic reasons? Or because strenuous yoga in their exquisitely decorated Tibetan meditation room had allowed them to transcend the body's clumsier functions? (Their house was so spotless, and so filled with New Age spirituality books, that I'm convinced it was the latter.)

There's no need for me to pry in medicine cabinets or nightstands: I'll find out everything I could want to know in your pantry. For an example, the fact that the children whose lacrosse photos cover the door of your fridge are swooningly in love with ranch dressing, and that you and your organic vegetables have made peace with this. Or that someone in your house has high hopes for gluten-free brownie mix but hasn't yet purged the pita chips.

Do you really eat this much quinoa? Does anyone? Or have you just convinced yourself you do, so that every time you go to the store you're sure to restock what's still previously untouched? There will almost always be three different ways to make coffee, from pour over to an unused French press and a streamlined pod machine, but only if you are over 60 (or possess Midwestern in-laws) will there be a Bundt pan. I'll find the lady of the house's stash of Luna bars and dry-roasted almonds. I know about the lone bottle of Coors hidden behind the half-drunk energy waters. If you last bought baking powder in 1998, I'll know it.

Slipping into the lives and sheets of others, I've relished the chance to feed goats, collect fresh eggs and wake up on a houseboat surrounded by a gang of raucous seagulls. The keys I've carried have revealed houses with swaying hammocks, disco-lit hot tubs and porches shaded with drooping fig trees. It's a glimpse, however temporary, into the dollhouse of another life.

When I step back through my own doorway, I see what I've created through fresh eyes, the dust of familiarity rubbed off. What would a stranger say about this tumbled bed scattered with novels, newspapers and stray pajamas, and surrounded by precariously stacked books and forgotten teacups? Wrapped in its ramshackle, welcoming embrace, I love it not because it's perfect, but because it's home. ○

*Stephanie Rosenbaum is a food writer and frequent house sitter whose work has been nominated twice for a James Beard Journalism Award. Her most recent books are* World of Doughnuts *and* The Art of Vintage Cocktails. *She lives in San Francisco.*

# SINGLE SERVINGS

WORDS BY NILS BERNSTEIN & PHOTOGRAPH BY ALICE GAO

*Just because you're eating alone doesn't mean you should be stuck with a frozen burrito or a sad salad. Here's an essay (and some recipes) to encourage you to whip up a decadent three-course meal for you and only you.*

In famed food writer M.F.K. Fisher's essay "On Dining Alone," she recounts the story of the Roman Empire gastronome Lucullus who, when his servant defended serving a modest meal because there were no dinner guests, admonished, "It is precisely when I am alone that you require to pay special attention to the dinner. At such times you must remember that Lucullus dines with Lucullus."

You should never think that cooking for yourself means there's no one to impress. Things that feel too extravagant or stressful for four—caviar or steak—are perfect for one: six oysters are a treat, 24 a chore. Some dishes—risotto, stir-fries or spaghetti carbonara—are best when made in single portions. If you love to experiment in the kitchen, it's a time to try tricky dishes and techniques—such as spatchcocked chicken, béarnaise sauce, soufflé or caramel—in the safety of your own private sanctuary.

This is also when you should enjoy those favorite dishes your loved ones don't care for (M.F.K. Fisher would take the opportunity to break out the canned shad roe, for an example). Rules go out the window: Eat breakfast for dinner, overdress your salad, have dessert first. As there's no one to witness your eating habits, you can enjoy some decadent culinary indulgences hunched over the sink as your amuse-bouche, such as a ripe mango slurped from its tenacious pit, sliced summer tomatoes or too much Gorgonzola on toasted pumpernickel.

For the delivery-prone, there are ways to make the idea of cooking solo seem less daunting: Choose dishes that can be prepped ahead of time and finished in the oven, preferably cooked in its serving dish, like a small iron skillet or an oversize ramekin; use recipes as inspiration rather than doctrine, as repeatedly dividing ingredient lists by four is a drag; and shopping at farmers markets can spark creativity while allowing you to buy only what you need, and also at peak quality.

Still, like cashmere baby clothes or a manual typewriter, pleasure—not practicality—is the goal when throwing a dinner party for one. Don't worry about making extra in order to have leftovers (there's something naughty about making a single serving of soup from scratch). Why not make several tiny dishes for an antipasto platter, or two desserts if you can't decide between fruit or chocolate? You can fiddle leisurely around the kitchen all day or prep everything early and spend the rest of the afternoon reading cookbooks in bed.

When it's time to eat though, take a break from your usual take-out tablescape. Even if it's your coffee table, set it with linens, your favorite dishes, a loose flower arrangement, beautiful bread and crisp radishes with the best butter and salt. Play lively music, but nothing too melancholy or loaded with nostalgia (try mariachi, LCD Soundsystem or '60s French pop). Serve yourself in multiple courses. Eat slowly. Bathe. And Lucullus would want you to turn off your phone. ○

*Nils Bernstein works by day as a music publicist for one of America's finest indie labels. His writing has appeared in* Bon Appétit, Men's Journal *and* Wine Enthusiast. *He lives in New York but escapes to Mexico City every chance he gets.*

SINGLE SERVINGS

# APPETIZER: OYSTERS AND MIGNONETTE

RECIPE & FOOD STYLING BY MARÍA DEL MAR SACASA
PHOTOGRAPH BY ALICE GAO & PROP STYLING BY KATE S. JORDAN

Oysters make the perfect personal indulgence: You can buy them in small quantities, and they're ideally accompanied by a sneaky glass of prosecco. (Beware: Oysters are full of good stuff, but they won't make you immune to hangovers.) For more of a challenge, buy unshucked oysters and spend an additional 20 minutes wrestling with them in the privacy of your kitchenette.

Competitive oyster shuckers may be able to shuck a dozen per minute, but we're in no hurry. Despite the threat of flying shell shards, spraying juice and physical injury, shucking oysters can be quite meditative once you get the hang of it. Just buy a few extra—some can be annoyingly tight or brittle, and even if they all open perfectly, no one's ever complained about extra oysters.

Cover your hand with a folded dish towel and place the rinsed oyster on it with its cupped side down and hinge pointing toward you. With an oyster knife (these only cost a few dollars, but a flat-head screwdriver will do in a pinch), work the tip in between the top and bottom shells near the hinge. Be patient, and feel free to look for better "entry points" elsewhere along the seam. Twist the knife to pop open the top shell. Cut the oyster free of the top and bottom shells, taking care not to lose any of the valuable oyster liquor. Remove any bits of shell, then flip the oyster for the best presentation.

---

*1/2 dozen oysters, shucked and
left on the half shell*

*1 medium shallot, very finely chopped*

*1/4 cup (2 ounces/60 milliliters)
Champagne vinegar*

*Freshly ground black pepper*

---

METHOD Arrange the oysters on a plate, over seaweed if desired. In a small bowl, combine the shallot, vinegar and pepper and allow to stand for about 10 minutes. Serve alongside oysters.

To make a green mignonette, add 1 tablespoon of very finely chopped flat-leaf parsley and substitute the Champagne vinegar with red wine vinegar. ○

*Serves 1*

# MAIN COURSE: SIMPLE CORNISH HEN WITH MUSHROOMS

RECIPE & FOOD STYLING BY MARÍA DEL MAR SACASA

PHOTOGRAPH BY ALICE GAO & PROP STYLING BY KATE S. JORDAN

**W**hen you don't have a neurotic housemate or partner to do the dishes for you, one-pan meals cut down on cleaning time. Use the leftovers (if there are any) as a simple salad or sandwich filling the next day, or eat them straight from the tupperware as a late-night snack.

*1 Cornish hen (about 600 grams)*

*3 tablespoons (45 grams) unsalted butter, at room temperature*

*1 tablespoon fresh herbs, such as thyme and sage, chopped*

*1 tablespoon (15 milliliters) olive oil, plus additional as needed*

*8 ounces (240 grams) mixed mushrooms, such as maitake and shiitake, torn into pieces with stalks removed*

*Salt and freshly ground black pepper*

**METHOD** Adjust an oven rack to the middle position and preheat the oven to 400°F/200°C.

Rinse the hen, remove and discard the giblet bag (or reserve for other use) and pat dry with a paper towel. Turn the hen breast side down on a cutting board and, with kitchen shears, cut close and parallel to the backbone, first on the right side of it, then to the left. Discard the backbone.

Turn the hen breast side up and press down on it with your palm to flatten. This process is called spatchcocking.

Gently run your fingertips under the skin to separate it from the meat. Season the hen with salt (3/4 teaspoon per 1 pound/450 grams is a good rule of thumb for all poultry) and pepper, rubbing it directly onto the meat and sprinkling a bit on top. Combine half of the butter with the herbs and pat it between the skin and flesh.

Combine the remaining butter and olive oil in a large skillet and heat over medium-high heat until just beginning to smoke. Cook the hen skin side down until deep golden, about 8 to 10 minutes. Using tongs, turn the hen skin side up and cook for 5 minutes. Transfer to the oven and roast until an instant-read thermometer registers 155°F/70°C, about 25 minutes. Transfer the hen to a serving platter, plate or carving board and allow to rest for a few minutes.

Take this time to prepare the mushrooms in the empty skillet. If the skillet looks dry, add a splash more olive oil. Add the mushrooms, season with salt and pepper and cook, stirring until golden, about 7 minutes. Enjoy the mushrooms with the hen. ○

*Serves 1*

# DESSERT: APPLE BLUE CHEESE BREAD PUDDING

RECIPE & FOOD STYLING BY MARÍA DEL MAR SACASA

PHOTOGRAPH BY ALICE GAO & PROP STYLING BY KATE S. JORDAN

D epending on your level of carb-indulgence, it can be difficult to polish off a whole loaf of bread solo before it gets stale. This recipe offers a clever way to use those chewy end bits before they go bad, fusing them with something you're meant to let grow pungent.

---

*1 tablespoon (15 grams) unsalted butter, softened*

*2 large eggs*

*1/4 cup (60 milliliters) whole milk, plus more as needed*

*1/4 cup (50 grams) granulated sugar*

*Pinch of salt*

*1 thick slice of bread or 2 small rolls, torn into pieces*

*1 small apple or pear, cored and diced*

*1 ounce (30 grams) blue cheese, such as Stilton or Gorgonzola dolce, crumbled*

*Honey and sea salt for topping*

---

METHOD Adjust an oven rack to the middle position and preheat the oven to 400°F/200°C. Rub an 8-ounce/250-milliliter-capacity, oven-safe ramekin with the butter.

Whisk the eggs, milk, sugar and salt together in a medium bowl. Add the bread, apple and cheese, and stir to combine, making sure the bread is properly soaked. If it looks dry, add a splash more milk. Scrape the mixture into the prepared ramekin, then place it on a small baking sheet to catch any drips.

Bake until the top of the pudding is set, about 30 minutes. Remove and allow to cool for about 5 minutes before eating. Drizzle with honey and sprinkle with sea salt to taste.  ○

*Serves 1*

# THE MODERN NOMAD

WORDS BY NABIL SABIO AZADI & PHOTOGRAPH BY TEC PETAJA

*For most people, the idea of home revolves around settling down in one place for a long time. For others, it's a state of mind rather than any particular city. One nomad-at-large reflects on how he came to live his life while constantly on the move.*

I have always explained myself as an Iranian–New Zealander: calling myself anything else feels like something important is missing. I owe my extreme sense of fluidity around the idea of home to my parents and their own extreme journey. They were born in the mid-'50s in Iran. Apparently people were afraid to clap on their wedding night because shells were being fired in the streets nearby and they didn't want to reveal the location of their happy gathering.

The revolution that would later radically alter the country's course was brewing, and in 1979 they escaped to Venezuela. They arrived knowing one phrase in Spanish (*Viva Venezuela!*), learned the language, gave birth to my older brother and made things work as best they could despite their own poverty and economic conditions. Hoping to move somewhere with a more stable political environment, they simultaneously applied for visas in Iceland and New Zealand. The latter's government responded first, and so it was that I was born a Kiwi.

As a child, the multicultural city of Auckland certainly felt like home and it still does above any other place. I spent my time equally with white New Zealanders, Iranians, Maori, Samoans, Tongans, Cook Islanders, Chinese and Indians. My parents' story, along with being raised in this environment, inadvertently taught me that roaming was growing, and this has had a tremendous influence on me.

The first time I traveled on my own, I was 13 years old. I had saved for a long time to go to England and France to "visit" my older brother via a mix of piano lessons and local photography assignments. I was gone for about a month and found ways of playing my London-based sibling off my parents so I could spend more time in Paris on my own. A disregard for personal safety has always been part of my personality.

Since then, I've traveled across the US, Israel, New Caledonia, New Zealand, Australia, the United Arab Emirates, Iran, France, Spain, the UK, Italy, Belgium, India, Morocco, Iceland, South Korea, Malaysia and more. Base camp would probably be Brisbane, Australia, where my family moved when I was 14. Since then, the longest I've been in one place has been seven months, but I normally swap cities every month or two. Everything I own would fit rather snugly in a sedan and most of what I keep can still come with me without exceeding baggage limits. I give a lot away.

People often use the term "nomad" when referring to me but I've never really responded to it. For me, traveling is just an amplified version of how I live my internal life. *Home* is a very special and strange word and, in the end, my concept of it has nothing to do with where I sleep.

When you spend your life traveling, you learn how much further you can push yourself. The other day my sister said to me, "The only people who found the edges of the world never lived to tell the tale." I often wonder about where those edges lie. I suspect seeking out magic is in some way why I've traveled as much as I have. ○

*Nabil Sabio Azadi is an artist who works in photography, sculpture and furniture. His first book,* For You the Traveller, *is a limited-edition guide to the world.*

# FORGOTTEN FIXTURES

---

*Haven't touched that salad spinner in a while? Household objects have feelings too. Here's what some of them might be feeling when you neglect them.*

---

LIMERICKS BY GEORGIA FRANCES KING & ILLUSTRATIONS BY KATRIN COETZER

### IN THE DARK

It's been weeks since I touched your finger
But my feelings for you still do linger
You started to scoff
Turning me on and off
You claimed illness, but I fear you malinger

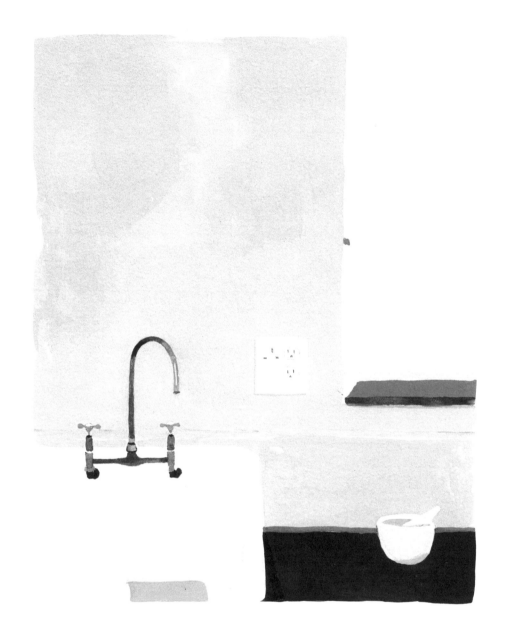

**EVERYTHING BUT THE KITCHEN SINK**

My insatiable thirst you can't drink
Only at home wares do you ever wink
I watch you wrestle
With that damn mortar and pestle
While my tears drip drip drip in the sink

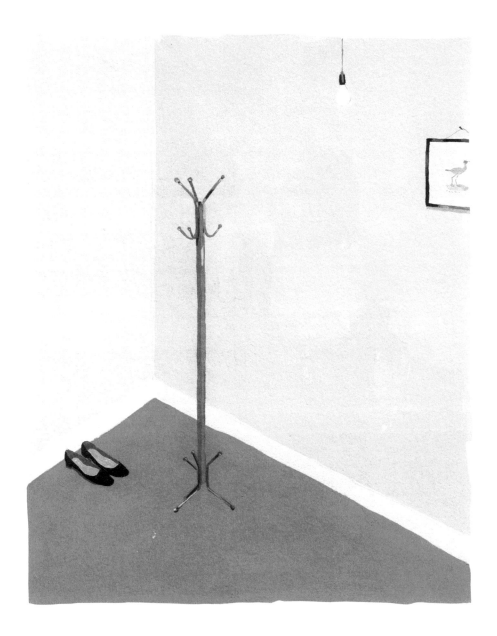

**STILL HANGING ON**

It was love the first time I looked
But you told me your heart was prebooked
By the closet down the hall
Where you instead hang your shawl
Yet I'm completely and utterly hooked

**YOU'RE BLINDS TO ME**

When I opened up, our love was lineal
But our relationship has since become trivial
I shield you away
From the brightness of day
So it hurts when you call me material

**DEAR JOHN**

I'm much more than you think I can be
Only the mailman understands me
I'm more than an opening
And really am hoping
That one day a letter will come just for me  ○

# MAKING A MOVE

---

*Moving is hard work. We're hoping these dashing photos help you forget that sweaty, stressful, dusty reality. We've also included some housewarming and housecooling party ideas to mark the occasion of leaving one home and setting up house in another.*

---

WORDS BY GAIL O'HARA & PHOTOGRAPHS BY LEO PATRONE

## HOW TO HAVE
## A HOUSECOOLING

**HOST** Chances are, when you're preparing to move, many of your friends may be conveniently out of town. Nevertheless, we like the idea of making an occasion out of getting ready to leave a place where you've spent some important time. It may be sad if you loved your home and neighborhood like crazy, or perhaps you're thrilled to be leaving the ants, bad plumbing and nosy neighbors behind. Either way, it will be emotional. Invite only your favorite people. Clean up so everyone can floor-sit comfortably. Spend your last few hours here in a melancholy haze, remembering the best of times and the worst of times. Every well-loved house deserves a proper send-off.

**GUESTS** Your friend is moving! Wear something casual in case you spend time sitting in dust bunnies or doing some last-minute packing. Bring something for everyone to snack on, and offer to help finish up late-breaking tasks such as touching up chipped paint, wrestling with an overgrown freezer or carrying a sad old couch to the curb. If it's going to be a late night, bring some cold-brew coffee. If it's going to be a sad one, try to make it a happy occasion by toasting your pal with some sparkling wine or cider.

**STUFF YOU'RE GETTING RID OF** Personally we recommend never getting rid of anything, but sometimes it's got to be done. The ideal time for a housecooling is when the movers have come, the big stuff is gone and you and your mates can play with the leftover boxes. Build a fort! Make cardboard sculptures! Hide the cat! If you do have stuff left, this is a great time to divvy it up: Make one area for things anyone can take, one area for things you'd like to donate and one area for things you'd like to trash. Tell your guests to bring giant IKEA bags with them so they can stuff them full of things you no longer want. Selling some vintage vinyl or fancy frocks? Have some change on hand and decide on prices ahead of time. You don't have to advertise this event as a sale, but if you have stuff to sell, make it clear!

**SNACKS** At this point you may have packed up your Le Creuset and antique cutlery, so it might be best to provide (or encourage others to bring) easy stuff that can be eaten off paper plates: cheese, salami, crudité, hummus and pita, big crusty bread and so on. Ordering a pizza would be smart. Ordering 10 would be smarter! If you're lucky enough to live in New York City, you can order anything on earth. Either way, keep it simple and have some napkins, plastic cups and forks on hand.

**PLAYLIST** Songs about moving, leaving and getting out of town would be ideal, even if they make you a bit nostalgic. Listen to the Madness tunes "Keep Moving" and "Our House," the Raincoats' album *Moving* or Chet Baker's "Leaving."

## HOW TO HAVE
## A HOUSEWARMING

**HOST** Housewarming parties are all about welcoming your pals and showing them your new place. It's not about getting free stuff and it's a bit sad to go so far as to request items, expect gifts or (god forbid) register for them. Make sure no one feels present pressure. (They'll probably bring one anyway.) You might have 972 followers on Facebook and 278 on Instagram, but you don't have to invite them all to your housewarming; just keep it small and simple and invite your real-life mates who'd actually want to come, and maybe a few new neighbors if they seem up for it. Show them around! If people offer to bring something, suggest simple stuff like bread, cheese and fruit.

**GUESTS** It may be a housewarming, but you should feel no pressure to bring a gift. It would be sweet and smart to bring *something*, just as you would bring to a non-housewarming event (at least something like a mammoth bar of dark chocolate filled with hazelnuts or a decent Pinot Noir). A housewarming should be about you and your relationship with the host, who is inviting you because they adore you. If you want to be a charming guest, bake a pie, make muffins or mix a giant vat of punch in vessels to leave behind. No host could resist freshly baked mac and cheese in a leave-behind Danish pan. A hunk of Tomme de Savoie is also always welcome.

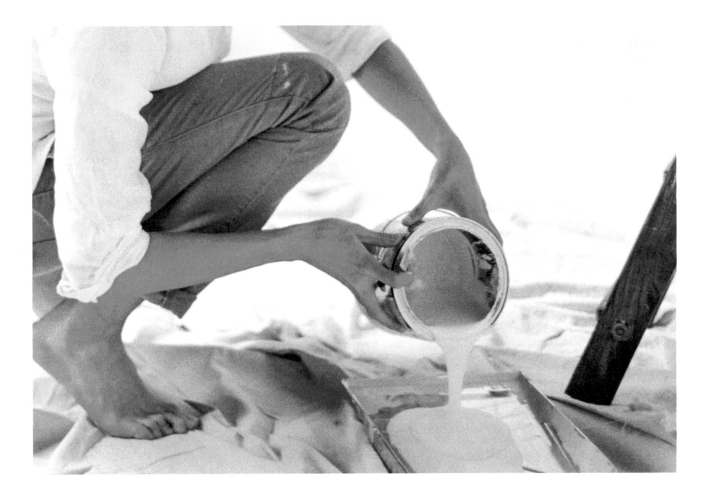

**GIFTS** Regardless of the advice previously given, many of you will still want to bring gifts. What you should give depends on who the host is. Is it your niece who just finished college and is getting her first apartment? She probably needs everything; ask her what she wants and chances are she'll love it. Is it a friend who just got married for the third time? They shouldn't be cheeky enough to expect anything after all those wedding gifts. Is the host your elderly aunt? She may have just unloaded a lot of worldly possessions and might not want any new ones! In this case, offer to help her do things around the house (hang photos, put boxes in the attic, clean out hard-to-reach corners) or bring something edible or beautiful (succulents, homemade granola, fresh herbs). The things everyone seems to toss and replace upon moving can sometimes be practical and boring, but most would be stoked to receive them: bread tins, cookie sheets, a big basket of organic condiments, extra-virgin olive oil and balsamic vinegar, fresh spices to populate the spice rack, baking ingredients, a nice vintage mixing bowl full of fresh fruit, herbs, giant bouquets of flowers, small houseplants or tiny trees would be ace. Failing that, craft beer, top-notch coffee, organic tea or a nice bottle of wine are all good. A metal bucket filled with eco-cleaning ingredients (baking soda, white vinegar, salt, lemons) would likely come in handy as well. For your foodie pals, impractical edible items such as Himalayan salt, salted caramel or elk jerky would be adored.

**PLAYLIST** Songs about houses, warmth and heat, such as Talking Heads' "Burning Down the House," Dizzy Gillespie's "Hot House" and Dionne Warwick's "A House Is Not a Home." ○

*Gail O'Hara is the managing editor at* Kinfolk. *A former editor at* SPIN, ELLEgirl *and* Time Out New York, *she also publishes* chickfactor. *She lives in Portland, Oregon.*

# TWO

ENTERTAINING FOR TWO

o  o

# LIVING FOR TWO: MAKE IT A DOUBLE

WORDS BY GEORGIA FRANCES KING & PHOTOGRAPH BY RYAN BENYI
SCULPTURE BY FRANCES PALMER

*Homes can be full of all kinds of couples: twos that share friendships,
twos that share beds, twos that share playdates and many more.
Pairing up can cause complications, but it also comes with its rewards.*

Although mathematicians may disagree with my hypothesis, there's more than one way to make two. Within a home, the one-plus-one equation may yield the same result—two toothbrushes, one house—but there are many calculations of people, partners and critters that can produce a domestic duo.

Living with your best friend is a thrilling blur of wine and melodrama. My first experience ended abruptly when my roommate was whisked away so swiftly by her job that she left the candles in her bedroom burning. This was my introduction to the greatest peril of living as a two: how quick and easy it is to suddenly become a one again. (And how empty your home can look without half of its furniture.) A few more couches graced that apartment, its doors revolving like the incongruous spiral staircase that led to its second floor. In the good times it was all in-jokes and Sunday baking sessions, and in the bad times there was always a shoulder to whimper on and someone to fetch another pint of ice cream.

When you share a place with a friend, there are certain unspoken rules that keep your lives independent—the closed doors at night, the splitting of pantry items, the blind eyes turned to midnight trysts—but once you've hung your boyfriend's underwear to dry in your living room, that line is well and truly eradicated. It's the tipping point when *mine* turns to *ours,* and when foreign teeth marks begin appearing in hunks of cheddar. My last experience of nesting was marred by a shoulder surgery that left my partner morphined up to his eyeballs and unable to put on his own pants. I'd tie his shoes, wash his hair, cook his dinner and cut his fingernails. With no one else home to look after him, I became both his savior and the reminder of his weakness. I hated it, but I loved him. The house became a battleground of discarded socks and, eventually, hearts.

Living with your loved one means compromise. You learn to let down facades and be dependent enough to need each other, but sovereign enough to still be yourself. The stakes are as high as your winter gas bill: You don't want to let yourselves become truly one, because if they ever depart, then you're left with only a half.

That's how I've found myself living in my current kind of twosome: with an adoring rescue kitten as demanding and precocious as a toddler. I certainly don't live alone: alone implies there's a singular presence in the house when, going by our collective hair in the sink and half-eaten cans of communal tuna, that number is a plural. Instead of waking up to my housemate's alarm clock through thin wooden walls or the grunt of a masculine snore, I'm raised by a shard of dawn light peering through my curtains and a small paw padding at my ear lobe, requesting breakfast.

Perhaps I'm substituting my desire to be needed by somebody again with a pooper-scooper. Or maybe a four-legged housemate is easier to unconditionally bond with than one who leaves the toilet seat up. But what I know now is that being part of a two gives you someone to come home to, whether it's to support, nurse or snuggle. Because without them, what would home be? ○ ○

*Georgia Frances King is the editor of* Kinfolk *and the scratch-covered mother of Pollyanna, a six-month-old feline bundle of claws and love. Originally from Melbourne, Australia, she now resides in Portland, Oregon.*

# THE HOUSEGUEST'S HANDBOOK

WORDS BY JULIE POINTER & PHOTOGRAPH BY LEO PATRONE

*A bad houseguest makes an impression as well as a mess.
We compile a list of ideas that will make your next experience
as a temporary lodger memorable for all the right reasons.*

Let's admit it: Having houseguests can be a challenge. In spite of our best intentions to eternally extend the warm hands of hospitality to friends, opening both our doors and spare bedrooms to weary travelers, it can be downright exhausting to surrender your personal sanctuary to the whirlwind of someone else's idiosyncrasies.

While we can't change the sometimes annoying habits of those we invite into our homes, we *can* allow the lessons we learn to alter the way we bunk up at friends' or families' houses ourselves. There's an art to being a good houseguest and it takes some diligent practice to get it just right. Next time you're taking advantage of the kindness of others—whether it's in the form of a couch or their backyard cottage—take heed of these suggestions for dwelling well.

**TRY TO CONTAIN YOURSELF** You may be the queen of your own personal castle, but in someone else's abode you must forfeit the freedom to distribute bits and pieces of your being around the premises as you please. Keep your belongings in one place, and for heaven's sake, be tidy.

**BE AN EMPATHETIC LODGER** Put yourself in the house slippers of your host (not literally) and visualize what might make you the most agreeable, generous guest. Close doors quietly when others are sleeping. Tread lightly in the morning. And, at the risk of being too graphic, clean the hair out of the tub.

**PITCH IN FOR MEALS** This might involve making a trip to the grocery store to stock up on eggs, coffee, artichokes and whatnot, chopping onions for dinner or washing the dishes after breakfast. Your participation in household affairs should be proportionate to the length of your stay. Do whatever you can to lighten the burden of another body (or several) in the house.

**BE REASONABLE ABOUT EXPECTATIONS** Take the harder, more humble approach and recognize that your host has a whole litany of responsibilities, worries and distractions that extend beyond merely satisfying your comforts. So commit to being flexible before you even step foot in the door. Also, be forgiving.

**PRACTICE COMMUNICATING WELL** In fact, perhaps even learn how to *over*communicate. This might be the key for getting off to a good start, as well as maintaining peace for the whole duration of your stay. Even if you're not a planner, figure out a strategy for letting your hosts know when they might expect you in and out of the house. If you say you're coming home at 10 p.m., don't waltz in the door at 2 a.m. with no warning and expect a warm greeting.

**COME BEARING GIFTS** A multitude of sins can be covered with the gracious offering of a thoughtful thank-you token. For the homebody, maybe some tea and a candle. For the home chef, a new cookbook or a jar of that fancy saffron you know they've been wanting to try. For the writer, a nice pen and delicate paper. It means something to express your gratitude in tangible ways as well as spoken.  ○ ○

*Julie Pointer is the community director at Kinfolk. She is a maker, writer and stylist living in Portland, Oregon, dreaming of one day running her own inn and artist retreat.*

# AN AMERICAN IN PARIS

WORDS BY CATHLEEN BOYDRON & PHOTOGRAPH BY KATHRIN KOSCHITZKI

*When Cathleen Boydron moved to Paris from the Midwest in 1986, she discovered the meaning of food. Now a trained chef who teaches cooking classes, she has adapted her food philosophy (and home cooking) to the dinner table–focused way of life en Français.*

**HOME ENTERTAINMENT** Traditionally, the French invite people into their homes for a meal and not to a restaurant; the home is the place where family and friends get together around the table. They'll spend a considerable amount of time planning, shopping and preparing a meal for guests—potluck doesn't really have a meaning here. I love to invite friends over for dinner or a Sunday lunch.

**REAL FOOD** I discovered what food actually was when I moved to France! I suddenly realized it was not just made to fill up my hungry stomach but could be associated with extreme pleasure, sharing, conversation and the discovery of new tastes. The possibilities were endless.

**THE FRENCH HOUSE** My home is a turn-of-the-century town house that was built in 1890. It's in a Parisian suburb just west of the city and has all of the features known in homes at that time: molding on the ceilings, fireplaces, oak floors and a vast oak staircase. I moved out of Paris when my third child was born to have a larger space and a backyard. My children are a bit older now, but I still love being so near to the city without the inconveniences.

**SLOW DOWN, SIT DOWN** Actual mealtimes—family mealtimes—are still very important in France. It might be simple and quick on weeknights but there's an actual break in the day for meals: They set a tempo to the day. The table is set and everyone eats together. Good table manners are still greatly appreciated here, and children are often being reprimanded because they have their elbows on the table or are using their knives with the wrong hand!

**DAILY DINNERS** I cook daily for my family, always something market fresh. Even though the amount of time French people dedicate to preparing meals has really changed, especially on a weekday, the whole idea of a meal is still extremely important to them.

**THE HOME COOK** Giving cooking lessons out of my home is something I really love to do. My goal is to show my students that, with a few techniques, they can really build up their confidence and make a wonderful meal, whether it's for a weeknight family dinner or a sophisticated Saturday reception. My home cooking for everyday is much less elaborate than what I teach in my classes. I probably use more fresh herbs, condiments, spices and citrus for my home meals, whereas in my classes we work quite a bit on wonderful and classic sauces. It's always good to know how to succeed in making a real *beurre blanc*, *béarnaise* and white wine sauce.

**MARKET STOCK** Get out to your local market as often as possible. Try to stay away from supermarkets because the seasons are all confused in them. Keep daily meals simple but make them fabulous by using the freshest ingredients available. And don't be afraid to use a little fresh cream and butter. ○ ○

*After working as a chef for nearly two decades, Cathleen Boydron began a cooking company out of her kitchen, teaching classes and preparing meals. She now works at Cyril Lignac's cooking school in Paris.*

# YOUNG VEGETABLES IN TEMPURA

RECIPE BY CATHLEEN BOYDRON & PHOTOGRAPHS BY KATHRIN KOSCHITZKI

This tempura recipe is really simple. The trick is to use very cold sparkling water, which makes the batter lighter. All of the beautiful spring vegetables come from an amazing vegetable farmer near Paris named Joel Thiébaud. Seeing his fresh produce at the market is so inspirational. I especially love the zucchini flowers and the Chioggia beets because when you cut them you discover the beautiful pink circles. I like to put blue poppy seeds in the batter too: It gives a little more flavor and makes the vegetables look even more interesting.

### FOR THE YOUNG VEGGIES

*Baby turnips with part of their green tops*

*Pink radishes with tips*

*French green beans*

*Pencil carrots*

*Mini beets*

*Mini zucchini flowers*

*Edible flowers such as violets and pansies*

### FOR THE TEMPURA BATTER

*Generous 1/2 cup (100 grams) all-purpose flour or rice flour*

*1 lightly beaten egg*

*1/2 cup plus 2 tablespoons (150 milliliters) ice-cold sparkling water*

*3 tablespoons (20 grams) blue poppy seeds*

*2 quarts (2 liters) peanut oil for deep fat frying*

METHOD *For the batter:* Make the tempura batter in advance. Whisk together the flour and beaten egg. Slowly pour the ice-cold sparkling water and whisk briskly to eliminate the lumps. Add the poppy seeds and whisk again. Cover and then keep it in the fridge until ready for use.

*For the veggies:* Wash all of the vegetables well. Spring vegetables have a very thin skin and therefore don't need peeling, except for the beets.

Deep-fry the veggies just before serving. Wait until all of the guests arrive, disappear for a few minutes and come back with a heaping platter of golden tempura veggies.

Heat the peanut oil over medium-high heat in a heavy-bottomed pot with high sides or deep fat fryer to 350°F/175°C. Whisk the tempura batter and dip the vegetables in a few at a time. Use a fork or chopsticks to take them out of the batter to allow excess batter to drip off.

Place the veggies delicately into the oil, 4 to 5 at a time. Turn them around in the oil using a slotted spoon and cook until they are golden brown. Transfer them to a paper towel-lined plate. Sprinkle the fried vegetables with sea salt and serve immediately. They won't last long! ○ ○

*Serves 6*

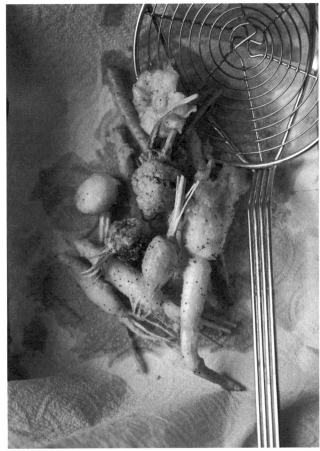

# CONTINENTAL DRIFT

---

*We ask three creative types to tell their stories of moving across the world,
leaving their home countries for an adventure abroad.*

---

ILLUSTRATIONS BY KATRIN COETZER

## EBONY BIZYS: SYDNEY > TOKYO

It took nine holidays trips to Tokyo before I decided that I might as well just move here. I had worked away in my little cubicle at *Vogue Living* magazine in Sydney for 11 years, and with the cut-off age for Japan's working holiday visa fast approaching, it was a case of now or never.

In June 2010, I arrived at my tiny 409-square-foot (38-square-meter) apartment in Shimokitazawa, Tokyo, which was a quarter the size of my previous living space. It surprised me just how easy it was to move yourself overseas: You follow a series of steps, redirect your mail, sort your belongings into boxes for storage and freight, throw a giant farewell party and all of the sudden you're writing a new return address on the back of your outgoing mail.

When I first walked in, I remember thinking how small, how Barbie doll–size it was: Ah, the trickery of fish-eye lens real estate photography. If I stand on my tiptoes, I can reach the ceiling. I have to bend down to wash the dishes. My toilet, in true Japanese style, has a tap on the top of it and a heated seat. I take my shoes off in my *genkan*. And I still struggle reading the *kanji* on the air-conditioner. But these odder aspects of daily life in Japan are what make it so incredibly exciting to live here.

From day one I set out to set up home. I bought a few quirky interior items such as a retro goose lamp and a pastel confetti system garland to help me miss my Australian furniture a little less. Other more formal things such as organizing national health insurance, getting a library card, finding a good English-speaking doctor and dentist… well, those took a little longer.

For me, it's the community-minded things that make Shimokitazawa more than just where I live, but my home. I'm friends with my post office lady. I chat about the weather with my Yamato and Sagawa courier men. I know where to get certain vegetables. I'm getting better at cupboard Tetris while jamming my craft materials behind Japanese sliding doors. And, on occasion, I drop a friendly *otsukaresama* ("good work!") beer to the owner of the small hairdresser at the bottom of my apartment block.

It's the small but beautiful daily moments like these that, without fail, make me smile at the fact that I'm able to live in this incredible city.

*Ebony Bizys is an Australian craft artist, designer and writer based in Tokyo. The founder of* Hello Sandwich, *she contributes to* Vogue Japan, *hosts craft workshops and has published numerous books and zines.*

## JOSUE MARTINEZ: GUATEMALA CITY > NEW ORLEANS > BALI

**U**ntil I was 18, the rhythm of Guatemala City's metropolitan valley kept me busy. My home was comfortable, warm and full of open doors to explore the infinity of my city's roads. From there I could see never-ending movement around tall buildings and busy streets, surrounded by beautiful mountains that separate the vast metropolis from untouched lands. It was in the streets of this valley I made my first close friends and also where I said my first farewells.

When college time hit, I followed my need to discover new worlds and picked a university in New Orleans, Louisiana. We didn't get along so well when I arrived there. At first it seemed like the options for entertainment were limited to night walks through touristy streets while listening to jazz and catching glimpses of the Mississippi River. But the more I explored the city, the more I felt like I belonged there: In the midst of nights filled with music and culinary experiences, this city taught me how a small place can be so full of secrets and how four years are never enough to get to know them all. As the months passed, strangers became acquaintances, classmates became colleagues and friends became family.

Toward the end of those years, I had to decide whether I wanted to go back to Guatemala or stay in New Orleans. I picked neither. Regardless of my love for both homes, I wanted to step out of what made me feel comfortable and find a new spot in the world. I accepted a job offer in Bali, Indonesia, where the traditional dances, palm trees and colorful clothes made me aware of how different the place is from anything I'd seen before. I'm getting used to long spells of hot weather that go beyond the humid season of New Orleans and the sunny days in Guatemala City. Every day I get to smell the flowers being offered to Hindu gods and the sound of prayers at noon. Going back to my native side of the world would take at least 15 hours and no less than a thousand dollars, but I don't have to worry about being far away from home. In only six months, I've found it again here.

New Orleans and Guatemala City are part of my past, but I still consider them home. I know I'll find family and friends there, ready to revive timeless memories and make new ones. Once a place gains the title of home, such a privilege is never taken away.

*Josue Martinez is a Guatemalan artist based in Bali, Indonesia. He currently teaches filmmaking and storytelling to children at an art school nestled between palm trees.*

## CARLY DIAZ: PORTLAND > AMSTERDAM > PORTLAND

In 2005, I left my home and family in the US to live abroad. I had whet my appetite with a summer in Rome and wanted to continue traveling. South Korea was first and then a year later the Netherlands, where I planned to remain in Amsterdam long enough to complete a two-year MA program and explore Europe in the process. But life often unfolds in the lines between carefully constructed plans.

Over the next seven years I ended up living in Amsterdam, I studied, worked, fell in love, rode my bike, shopped for groceries, paid my bills, went to the dentist, learned to speak functional Dutch, got married, filed taxes and all of the other exciting and unexciting details that make up life. Amsterdam became my home in the truest sense of the word. The moment my German husband and I started to contemplate leaving, I began to see everything I'd miss, from the easy way I could navigate the city on two wheels, the perfect size latte, my friends and all of the faces that became a regular part of my daily life, from the greengrocer to the postman.

Why leave a home we loved so much? Amsterdam was wonderful in many ways, but we missed the mountains and nature of our respective home countries. I longed for my family, sisters and rapidly growing nieces. Our dreams for the future saw us in India, Germany, Italy and England. But, for now, it was time to be in Portland, Oregon.

When we arrived in the spring of 2013, it took about two months for us to find a suitable apartment, start settling into new jobs, receive the shipping container that had transported our belongings across the ocean and start rediscovering Portland. Leaving home changes you. And when you come home, you and it are not the same. I wonder how long it takes for home to feel like home again?

It's not just the fact that we still don't have a couch, use cardboard boxes for nightstands and people question my accent: I've complicated the ideal concept of home by living in four countries over the past 10 years, by marrying someone born on another continent and by wondering where the next move will take us. Once the whole world becomes a possible place to reside, the sense of home undergoes a profound shift. I now turn to the people inside my home and within my community to create a place of love and connection, wherever in the world that might be.  ○ ○

*Carly Diaz is a creative director and content strategist with a love for the written word, visual storytelling and all things digital. She lives in Portland, Oregon.*

# GREAT DANES

*Scandinavian design makes us weak in the knees and has been able to stand the test of time. We check in with three Copenhagen creatives —a lighting designer, an architect and a furniture maker— to talk about Danish design, past and present.*

WORDS BY JOANNA HAN & PHOTOGRAPHS BY JONAS BJERRE-POULSEN

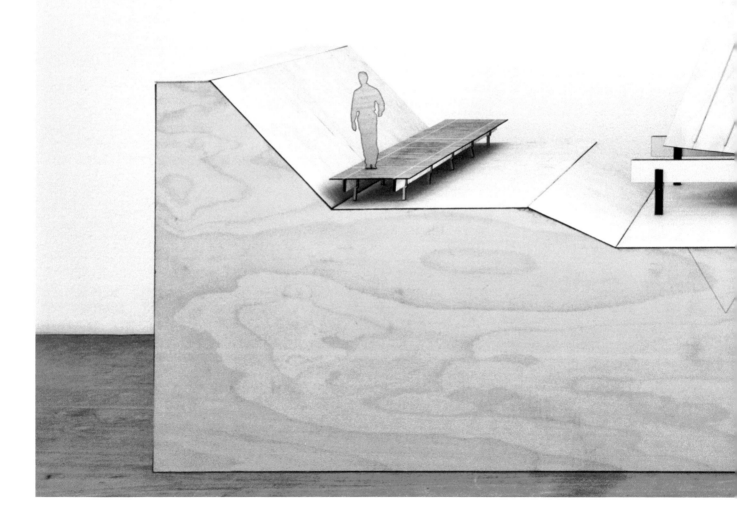

# THE LIGHTING DESIGNER

Afte studying at the top design schools in Copenhagen and Helsinki, Cecilie Manz has produced an impressive collection of award-winning furniture, objects and lighting, including her famous "Mingus" lamp. A recipient of the Thorvald Bindesbøll Medal, the Bruno Mathsson Prize and the Finn Juhl Prize, Cecilie works out of her Copenhagen studio with clients including Fritz Hansen, Lightyears, Bang & Olufsen and more.

### WHAT MAKES SCANDINAVIAN DESIGN SO APPEALING?

The '50s and '60s really were golden periods in Scandinavian design. The style had an impact because it was modern, sometimes radical and a fruitful collaboration between the carpenter and the designer. Designers believed in rational solutions and had visions that the everyday man in the street would be able to afford their furniture. It didn't really turn out that way, but that's a different story! This image of Scandinavia is still there, even though it's over now and IKEA is the dominant player.

### HOW DO YOU BALANCE FORM AND FUNCTION IN YOUR WORK?

The functional aspect comes first in the work process because it's the core of the object: What is its purpose? Is it for drinking, holding, sitting or something else? Shape, texture and material come next. Many people have this idea of designing as artsy doodles on paper that could end up being a chair or a lamp depending on how you turn the paper. It might be okay in spectacular architecture but it doesn't work that way for me. The hard part of designing is to solve the riddle—to get the "outer" to correspond to the "inner" in the most obvious and natural way.

### IS YOUR WORK INFLUENCED BY ANY NON-DESIGN ELEMENTS?

Everyday life is one of my biggest sources of inspiration—a classic answer, but still true. This is where I detect irritating details or smaller problems to be solved or maybe just improved slightly. A bike ride to work with music in my ears is good, or looking at colors in nature and museums in the cities I travel to.

### LIGHTING MUST BE MORE IMPORTANT FOR SOMEONE LIVING IN A REGION OF THE WORLD THAT'S DARK FOR HALF THE YEAR. WHAT EFFECT DOES THIS HAVE ON YOUR DESIGN PROCESS?

Light is very important, especially cozy, pleasant lighting. In Southern Europe they tend to hang fluorescent tubes from the ceiling—for convenience I believe—but it gives off a completely horrible light. By hanging pendants low, perhaps above a warm-toned surface like wood, the general coloring in the room gets warmer. And rather than only one light hanging too high, more light sources also help.

### HOW CAN PEOPLE CREATE A COMFORTABLE YET AESTHETICALLY PLEASING HOME?

Ask yourself what would really please you. You and your family are the ones living in your home, not your guests or a photographer—it should fit your own personal aesthetics and needs. Dare to be deadly boring!

# THE ARCHITECT

Jakob Olmo Ahlmann is an architect at Copenhagen-based architecture firm Tegnestuen Vandkunsten. A recipient of the Alvar Aalto Medal in 2009, the firm was recognized for nearly four decades of outstanding achievements in residential architecture with a focus on socially aware, convertible and sustainably developed works. Jakob specializes in housing and educational projects and is involved in all stages of the projects at the firm, from the first sketch to the final realization phase.

**WHAT'S YOUR TAKE ON THE CORRELATION BETWEEN DESIGN AND THE CONCEPT OF HOME?**

The concept of home is shaped by things with meaning, personal value, care, love and intention. So is good design. Cut away the needless.

**WHAT IS IT ABOUT SCANDINAVIAN DESIGN—AND DANISH DESIGN IN PARTICULAR—THAT PEOPLE FIND SO FASCINATING?**

The present Danish architecture scene points in too many directions to be generalized. But if I were to focus on one thing, it could be the notion of light. Since we have so little—especially in the wintertime—we are encouraged to give it special attention. We recently dealt with this in its most extreme context in our proposal titled "New Arctic Building Practice" for the Venice Biennale of Architecture. In the proposal, we wrap the housing units in a translucent greenhouse that invites the Northern light to enter in the wintertime where the sun never rises.

**WHAT'S THE RELATIONSHIP BETWEEN FORM AND FUNCTION IN YOUR WORK?**

If you come to the notion that form and function work at the expense of the other or need to be balanced, you might need to rethink your concept.

**DOES IT EVER FEEL LIKE IT'S DIFFICULT TO CREATE AND CONTRIBUTE SOMETHING NEW?**

We don't do new: We do in time, in place. Every project comes with a site, a client and a program. In that sense, every project is unique. If it makes sense in that understanding to reuse elements, details or ideas from other projects, we should do so. I always encourage reusing what is good as long as the copy is better than the original.

**WHEN DESIGNING A HOUSE, HOW DO YOU CONSIDER THE RESIDENTS' LIVES AND PERSONALITIES?**

I consider designing their house rather than their home—a good house can accommodate a thousand different homes over time. I believe in moveable walls and generous, welcoming and multifunctional rooms.

**HOW CAN PEOPLE CREATE A COMFORTABLE YET AESTHETICALLY PLEASING HOME?**

Push the project beyond the concept. Feel the materials, see the light, smell the coffee. And don't forget the storage space.

**WHAT ELEMENTS OF YOUR HOUSE MAKE IT FEEL LIKE A HOME?**

I try to surround myself with things of great importance to me. My two kids and my girlfriend make my home feel like home.

# THE FURNITURE MAKER

**C**hristina Liljenberg Halstrøm is known for her signature trio of materials: wood, leather and wool. She's worked for clients including Skagerak Denmark, Design Nation and Menu, and has shown in exhibitions across Northern Europe and beyond. As showcased in her "Cover Up" chair, Christina's distinctly clean style features muted grays, light woods and slim structures.

---

**WHY ARE PEOPLE SO OBSESSED WITH DANISH DESIGN?**

I guess we're very practical in Denmark and it's evident in the objects we design. Finding the most beautiful way to make an object very useful is a great challenge, but this is what Danish designers are really good at.

**HOW IS DESIGN CURRENTLY CHANGING IN THE FURNITURE INDUSTRY?**

The furniture business is very slow. New products can't hit the market at the same rate as for fashion, for an example, even though there's a demand for it. But this allows designers to dwell on details and try out many directions before deciding on the final draft. And why should we have to come up with something new? For me, objects don't always need to be completely new—it can be an improvement of a function we already know.

**AS SOMEONE WHO'S PART-DANISH AND PART-SWEDISH, DO YOU NOTICE ANY CHARACTERISTICS THAT DISTINGUISH BETWEEN THE TWO DESIGN AESTHETICS?**

Swedish designers aren't so afraid of decorations. The phrase "form follows function" is alive and well in Denmark, and while I'm almost mortally afraid of creating something that doesn't have a well-defined function, I very much enjoy the more conceptual approach that Swedish designers take.

**PLEASE DESCRIBE YOUR OWN HOME.**

I live with my husband and two boys in an apartment in Copenhagen. We have quite a lot of books, which are the main decoration. Actually, most things we have are functional objects! Until recently when my grandmother died, I never really had things sitting around just because they were beautiful: Now I have some Swedish horses on a shelf that remind me of my childhood summers in Sweden. I also have a lot of different chairs and stools. I wish I had more space.

**HOW CAN PEOPLE CREATE A COMFORTABLE YET AESTHETICALLY PLEASING HOME?**

Think about the people living in the home. If there are kids, maybe white couches are just a stressful element.

**IS YOUR WORK INSPIRED BY ANY NON-DESIGN ELEMENTS?**

I like to read. I find Gilles Deleuze and Jorge Luis Borges especially inspiring, and I read anything that has to do with Japan. For his PhD, my husband is studying rhetorical methods that can be used in the design process, and we've had some pretty nerdy conversations that have greatly influenced my work. ○ ○

*Joanna Han is the deputy editor at* Kinfolk. *She lives, writes and drinks good coffee in Portland, Oregon, but is scheming to move to Sweden.*

# A HOME AWAY FROM HOME

WORDS BY ROMY ASH & PHOTOGRAPH BY ADRIAN GAUT

*Travel can make you see the world in a different way, but it can also remind you of what you've left behind. Here are some ideas for things to bring along that will make you feel at home on the road.*

Traveling means leaving behind all that is familiar—that's really the point. I love that moment of landing somewhere new where everything is exciting and even going to the supermarket can be an adventure. There's a heightened awareness to the smells of a new place, to the light. But staying in foreign places can be disorienting. I travel a great deal—both for work and fun—but really, I'm a homebody. I like wherever I'm staying to have that feeling of home, even if I'm far away from my own.

A temporary room in a hotel, hostel or apartment can be transformed into a home with just a little thought. You don't have to carry your most treasured possessions with you, though you could. I've carried a teacup wrapped very carefully in a sweater and underwear at the bottom of my bag. It isn't even the cup itself that makes me feel at home: it's the familiarity of holding it. I find the roughness of a tiny chip in the handle deeply comforting, the weight of it in my hand. Here are some ideas of things to do when you arrive, to anchor you and make you feel more at home.

UNPACK YOUR BAGS IMMEDIATELY ON ARRIVAL Hide the empty luggage under the bed. This not only means your shirts will unwrinkle but that you're claiming your space. Your clothes are familiar, holding the scent of your perfume or aftershave. Even if the space has no wardrobe, at least hang your scarf and coat over the bed's headboard.

MAKE SOMETHING TASTY If you're lucky enough to be staying somewhere with a kitchen, cook a meal. When you're feeling homesick, whip up something familiar like a dish your mother used to make. Sometimes specific ingredients can be hard to find, so it might be better to go to a fresh produce market and use a recipe that works from the ingredients up. It's the act of cooking—the chopping and the stirring—that grounds you in a new environment.

BRING SOMETHING FROM HOME Take a pretty pillow to use while you travel or to throw on your bed when you arrive. It's something that is both practical and makes your room feel like home.

HAVE THE FIXINGS FOR COFFEE OR TEA There's comfort in the ritual. I like to carry tea and coffee with me, but if that's not possible, do a little research before you get there so you know where to go.

COLLECT A BOUQUET Pick some flowers, find a pretty shell on the beach or collect stones, seedpods or even a bunch of local grasses. It doesn't matter what as long as you bring something beautiful and natural inside. Hotel rooms are cleaned often, so it's nice to have a beautiful mess to give a space life.

TAKE OVER THE BEDSIDE TABLE Put something next to your bed, even if it's just a good book you're reading. That familiar book (or notepad) will be there when you go to sleep and again when you wake up.

LET THE SUNSHINE IN If it's summer then open all the windows too, because feeling at home is also about connecting with the present, bringing that new world in. ○ ○

*Romy Ash usually writes fiction. Her debut novel,* Floundering, *was published in 2012. She lives in Melbourne, Australia.*

# TOME SWEET TOME

WORDS BY DAVID WINWARD

*Is your home filled with floor-to-ceiling bookcases or is your entire library contained on a hard drive? No matter your page-reading preference, here are a few ways you can prepare your bookshelf for the digital age.*

Many people argue that print will never die, often ironically accompanied by a digital image of a print book, cup of tea, curtained window and a Hudson filter. Having a physical manifestation of books in your home is like having a physical manifestation of your wisdom, genius or intellect on display. But with the rise of digital reading, how can you possibly present your vast knowledge if it's not imposingly towering over people when they enter your home? In case the day of the e-takeover ever comes, here are some thoughts and benefits to incorporating digital books into your home.

**THE CASE AGAINST BOOKCASES** Displaying the books you own used to be a reflection of your wealth. If this sort of spectacle is at the top of your priority list, hook up your television or computer to show your e-book shelf. During private events, make a point to say, "That reminds me of a quote I read the other day," then look it up and display it on the screen. The problem with this method of exhibition is that people might think you are a little pretentious, but isn't that the point of large, publicly placed libraries anyway?

**SAVE THE WHALES VS. MOBY DICK** You've thought of yourself as an environmentally conscious person ever since writing an essay in elementary school about saving the whales. How can you have all of those print books displayed in your home and justify the destruction of all of those trees? The cost of printing a book is also much higher than creating a digital copy. Some people will argue that those trees were grown to make paper, but how many times have you argued against that exact line of thought regarding farm animals? If you're not quite ready to join the digital future, at least buy used books for your home library, which means the book itself is getting used more than once. Also, this will add to your intellectual credibility, as you'll never seem to be reading new fiction.

**OWNING LESS IS MORE** Material books have the disadvantage of being cumbersome physical objects, but your entire digital library could weigh less than your copy of *One Hundred Years of Solitude*. Many book lovers cannot control the impulse to purchase more: The fact that every bookshelf is already filled to capacity doesn't deter them from buying a new one, hiding the bookstore bags from their significant others. Bibliophiles tend to have tottering stacks of them on every available surface in their home. If this sounds like you, digital books may be just the thing to save you from dying alone under a toppled shelf while attempting to get your cat to alert the neighbors.

**AUDIBLE ADVANTAGE** Have your audio books playing like background music at different gatherings. Choose something fitting to the event: Emily Dickinson matches a dinner party, for an example, or Cormac McCarthy's *Blood Meridian* would be good if you feel the need to make strangers uncomfortable, making it perfect for when your daughter's date is picking her up for the dance. Being able to play your books out loud offers something that a physical book could never give. (That, and you can't stare daggers at your daughter's suitor while reading aloud.)

**TO READ OR NOT TO READ** Have you ever skipped a book because you were afraid of what people might think of you for reading it? A digital book is the perfect way to read whatever you want without feeling judged, just like the college student who tucks a comic inside his philosophy textbook. Now you can read trashy romance paperbacks, teen vampire novels or self-help books in public without shame or embarrassment. Let the mere fact you're reading be the only thing your fellow subway commuters know about you.

**FREE THE CLASSICS** Another benefit of digital books is that you can have a massive library without spending a cent—legally! You can download all of the classics that have fallen out of copyright for free at gutenberg.org: This way you're able to have a collection of volumes in the thousands without coughing up a dime. The trick is then to *read* these books. Nothing is worse than a person who has a large collection and doesn't read them.

**FOR THE LOVE OF TEXT** There's a light at the end of the computer-generated tunnel though. Whatever your opinion is on the print vs. digital divide, it has us thinking about reading again. In fact, the digital age may force us to learn to love books for their text and not their physical selves. Our homes may become book-less, but not our lives. So no matter the way you prefer to digest your nightly pages, remember the point of a book is in the reading of it. ○ ○

*David Winward is a writer moonlighting in a law office based in Salt Lake City, Utah. He is chipping away at his debut novel,* The Analects of Facetious (Bastard Brother of Confucius).

## A FURRY HOME COMPANION

*Who is the head of the household? Sometimes it's the humble house cat who watches over the place when you're out. One feline owner discovers how his own cat helped him see his home in a whole new way.*

WORDS BY TRAVIS ELBOROUGH &
PHOTOGRAPHS BY JAMES FITZGERALD III

Current scientific theory favors the notion that cats, once feral hunters, domesticated themselves. I'm not a scientist, but one thing I can say is that our cat domesticated *us*. It's fair to say my wife and I were certainly *aware* of our home in the couple of years we lived together before deciding to get a cat. But *aware* in the sense of *vaguely aware, kinda heard of.* We were familiar with our home in the way you can be familiar with the plot of a movie you dozed through one night on TV. We saw our apartment every day, of course, but we failed to notice much about it (apart from a few quirks with the plumbing that were all too difficult not to notice, unfortunately).

The arrival of Phoebe, a mackerel-striped tabby with a little brown nose and greener eyes than Kim Novak, a few days before Christmas changed all of that forever. For a start, the instant we opened the cat carrier, she squeezed herself behind a large and fully stocked bookcase. Safely ensconced there, she refused to come out. For the next two weeks, our home felt haunted. Every evening we'd put fresh food and water out for Phoebe and retire to bed, having failed quite miserably to coax her from her hiding place. Each morning though, we'd awake to find just a few crumbs left behind and a telltale trail of hairs all around the lounge.

At that point we became intensely aware of our home. We scrutinized furniture for the slightest cat scratches. The faintest sounds found us jumping from room to room in the hope of catching a glimpse of Phoebe. Eventually she emerged and began making her presence felt about the place, at first tentatively, and then quite tenaciously. Having hidden from us for so long, she now preferred to keep us in clear sight. She followed us into different rooms and liked to give our ankles a disobliging swipe whenever we opened the front door to leave the apartment.

Upon returning, we'd usually find her waiting on the hall mat with a somewhat accusatory expression, as if she'd waited all that time on the same spot for us to come home. And home we came because we had to for Phoebe's sake, since she never left the building. But, in fact, we longed to be at home. Because home was where Phoebe was.

Our apartment has become much more homey now that we have a feline who demands food and affection and savages rugs on an almost hourly basis. Our apartment genuinely feels more lived-in. Not only do we both spend more time here, but Phoebe—in treating it like her own personal hotel by wrecking carpets and hiding bathroom towels—has made us appreciate it as never before. Salvador Dalí once argued that the future of architecture lay in making soft and hairy homes. So perhaps all anyone needs is a cat: Certainly our home has never felt softer or been hairier since Phoebe came to live with us. And now we can't imagine it any other way. ○ ○

*Travis Elborough's most recent book,* London Bridge in America: The Tall Story of a Transatlantic Crossing, *was published by Jonathan Cape in 2013.*

# MAN ABOUT THE HOUSE

WORDS BY GAIL O'HARA & IMAGES COURTESY OF SIR TERENCE CONRAN

*Sir Terence Conran knows a thing or two about setting up a home. The 82-year-old designer has created hundreds of products, written more than 50 books and has had a huge impact on design. He tells us some stories from his decades sitting in the creator's chair.*

### WHAT WAS YOUR CHILDHOOD HOME LIKE?

I lived in several homes. Following the outbreak of World War II, the whole family left London for Old Shepherds Farm in Hampshire. My mother had very simple tastes that I suppose I inherited. I remember big, white, blocky, loose-covered linen sofas and chairs, as well as Dutch flower pictures. Money was very tight, so we didn't have luxuries, but she saw that my sister and I received the best creative education possible. It also encouraged my love of cooking and growing vegetables and herbs. We had a dairy, rabbits, pigs, geese and cart horses, which thankfully we didn't eat! I remember an extraordinary abandoned walled garden opposite where all kinds of tasty treats grew, such as peaches and loganberries.

### WHAT MAKES YOU FEEL AT HOME?

Being surrounded by the things I love that I've inherited or collected makes me feel at home. I used to be a collector of butterflies and moths, but now it's frowned upon. I once found a hawk moth so rare that I had a letter published about it in *The Times*—thrilling for a young boy. In my country home, I've mounted 19 Bugatti pedal cars on a wall as if they were moths.

### HOW DOES YOUR HOME REFLECT YOUR PERSONALITY?

That's the key—a home must always reflect your own personality and character, not some designer or decorator you've read about. Filling your room with things you love is what makes a house your home. I've always mixed antique and flea market furnishings with modern designs—this has been a trademark of Conran design and, of course, I practice what I preach!

### HOW DOES IT FEEL TO KNOW THAT YOUR DESIGNS ARE IN SO MANY HOMES?

At the risk of sounding big-headed, I believe it's the greatest pleasure of all and the biggest compliment a designer can receive. We didn't get into this business to win awards, earn pots of cash or collect titles; we just had a fundamental and fierce belief that good design gives people pleasure and improves the quality of their lives.

### WHEN YOU TRAVEL, WHAT DO YOU BRING ALONG THAT MAKES YOU FEEL AT HOME?

It might sound obvious, but cigars: I smoke four of them a day and find them even more pleasurable on holiday. I also take a camera with several white notebooks and lots of pencils so I can sketch ideas or images down to jog the memory. I love being a flaneur in a foreign town, absorbing the sights, sounds, smells, tastes and atmosphere of a place and meeting interesting new people.

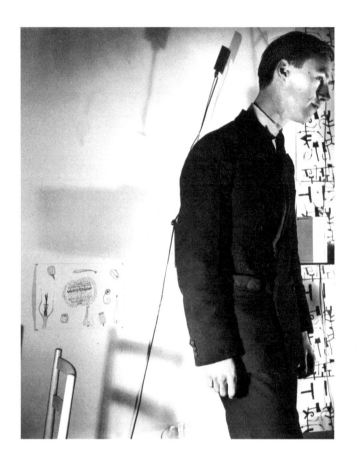

### WHAT COULD YOU NOT LIVE WITHOUT IN YOUR HOME?

We have an excellent wine cellar, a well-stocked pantry and a good Aga range to cook from, so we have everything we need. I couldn't live without a good set of knives for the kitchen though—those are a cook's basic necessity!

### WHAT AREA OF YOUR HOME DO YOU SPEND THE MOST TIME IN?

It may sound boring, but I have a large room in the country that I use as an office that's very personal, comfortable and creative. It's filled with books and models of my designs, pictures of family and friends, a huge desk, a comfortable sofa, an open wood fire and views over the fields and river. I love the energy of London, but Barton Court is where I have space to think, design and create.

### HOW HAVE YOU WATCHED DESIGN CHANGE OVER TIME?

I've lived with the changes rather than watched or observed them. My generation believed that good design could improve the quality of life for everybody because it gives you pleasure and makes life better through products or buildings that work well, are affordable and look beautiful. Good design is enduring and moves with the trends but is never held hostage by fashion or novelty. Think of a classic leather club chair, a pair of good shoes or an old pair of Levi's: These items look as good today as they did 50 years ago.

### WHAT HAVE BEEN SOME OF YOUR FAVORITE DESIGN PERIODS?

The work of midcentury modern designers—Eames, Saarinen, the Shakers—remains so popular because their work was brilliant and is as relevant today as it was then. It was a time of serious optimism, exploring revolutionary techniques in furniture making and design. As students in the late 1940s, midcentury modern design was our great inspiration. We learned of their work through a West Coast magazine called *Arts & Architecture*, which was a design bible for us at the time and had a huge impact on the European design world.

### WHAT ARE YOUR MOST PRIZED POSSESSIONS?

I've inherited some furniture that's more than 300 years old and I own my favorite chair: the Karuselli. The thing I like best is my collections, my little museums around the house. I particularly like my glass pieces: industrial glass, laboratory glass, 18th-century drinking glasses and agricultural pieces. I love their transparency, lightness and the traditional shapes.

### DO YOU EVER STOP WORKING WHEN AT HOME? WHAT DO YOU DO TO RELAX?

I'm very lucky in that practically everything I do in my business life I'd also do for pleasure: designing, writing, eating, drinking, shopping, traveling, reading, drawing, making furniture, throwing pots, gardening, even smoking my cigars. I always try to find the time to relax. Some things I like include fireworks, water mills, objects connected to travel from the 1920s and '30s, Japanese teahouses, butterflies, dragonflies, rivers and boats, jazz music and beautiful gardens.

### WHAT ADVICE DO YOU HAVE FOR PEOPLE SETTING UP A FIRST HOME?

In the long term, make sure you get the shell and services right before you consider the furniture or decoration. People all too often try to do everything all at once. Live with your home, understand it and gradually color and furnish it as you find out how you use it.

### WHAT DO YOU BELIEVE EVERYONE SHOULD HAVE IN THEIR HOMES?

Above all else, somebody they love. After that, plenty of things they love. ○ ○

# DREAMING IN CARDBOARD

*With no blueprints and building costs to worry about, a child's imaginary house is as whimsical as it comes. We asked some kids in London to describe their dream homes and then brought them to life.*

PHOTOGRAPHS BY NEIL BEDFORD & SET DESIGN BY HELEN MACINTYRE

"My house would be built in a giant tree with branches. There would be secret passages and trick doors, so the best game would be hide-and-seek because there would be lots of hiding holes in the trunk. And to stop the baddies from getting in, I'd create a special magic shield all around my house."

**THE TREE HOUSE, EMILY MAE, AGE 6**

"I would want my house to be a big pirate ship so I could sail across the sea all day. My friends would help me steer but I'd still be the Captain! We'd all play musical chairs on the deck when there aren't any bad guys to look out for. There'd also be a light on the front so Mom could always see where I am."

**THE BIG PIRATE SHIP, INDIGO, AGE 5**

"I'd like to live in a normal little cottage with flowers on the roof. I'd invite my friends over all the time to make daisy chains and play I Spy. It would also have a nice kitchen. My favorite thing to bake is cookies and my oven would be so big that I could make hundreds and share them all."

**THE FLOWER COTTAGE, WILLOW, AGE 6**

"Mine would be tall and made of lots of different shapes with a slide wrapping around the top to the bottom. It'd also be able to fly anywhere I want! I'd have magic shows in the attic for my little brother to watch and there'd be a telescope right at the top to watch the stars and planets at night." ○ ○

**THE PLANETARIUM, JAHMARI, AGE 7**

# FEW

ENTERTAINING FOR A FEW

○ ○ ○

# LIVING WITH A FEW: THE GROUP HOUSE

WORDS BY AMELIA SCHMIDT & PHOTOGRAPH BY RYAN BENYI
SCULPTURE BY FRANCES PALMER

*The shared house experience can be filled with stolen snacks, unpaid bills and filthy bathrooms. But, as our seasoned sharer explains, it can also mean finding a faux family who teaches you about something more than fridge politics.*

For many people, shared housing is a necessary evil—a temporary stopgap between your family's abode and home ownership. It's an experience often marked by college parties and sticky kitchen floors, broken bathroom fixtures and the destruction of personal property. But these days it seems sharing a house is turning into something much more than that. Maybe it has to do with the housing market and the job market being increasingly out of sync, or the settle-down-and-marry deadline moving further into the future. And, of course, there's that sneaky urban sprawl.

I guess that's why I'm still in a group house. After all, I have a steady job, haven't opened a textbook in a lifetime, own a French oven, have shared a room with my boyfriend and our cat for years in different group houses and we're even installing a home security system. But, if I'm really honest, I'm still living in a group house because it's what has helped craft me into who I am—for better or worse.

My older sister and I met in my first group house. We may not have been related by blood, but as the eldest sibling in my "real" family, I never knew the joys of hand-me-downs or enjoying a homemade dinner with people other than my parents. I learned you can eat the skin of a kiwi fruit and that a spoonful of sugar can make pasta sauce better. The lessons of adulthood included more than learning how to cook and eat, personal hygiene and basic appliance operation though. It has also taught me compassion and compromise, patience and responsibility.

Sharing a domestic setting with strangers gives you an insight into their personalities that can absolutely and definitely dictate whether you think they're decent human beings or not. Many folks come together in group houses in ways that many families may never achieve: A family living together is built around authority and parent-child power structures, but a shared house forces adulthood and responsibility onto each member of the group, requiring that each person participates, supports and forms at least some semblance of a friendship.

And then there are those situations that force you to come together regardless: the leaking roof and the flooding toilet; the neighbor's party complaints and the surprise home inspections; or the sudden death of a rabbit you were looking after for your traveling housemate and the guilt that follows such a nightmare.

A shared house is a shared experience—we share space, furniture and crockery, but more than that, we share friends, habits and experiences. Housemates are more than family, and group houses are much more than houses.

In *Four Quartets*, T.S. Eliot wrote, "Home is where one starts from." It fits with an idea I've always had that home, despite often being attached to a steadfastly stationary building, is a portable concept that travels with us, rather than with a geographical place. That's why my group house has a living room in Melbourne and a courtyard in Sydney, a kitchen in Erskineville and a fireplace in Brunswick. Because home *is* where you start from: It's where the story of your life begins. Each tale overlaps, weaves and combines together, like a cupboard of mismatched mugs. ○ ○ ○

*Amelia Schmidt lives at the edge of the city in Melbourne, Australia, in a converted stable with her boyfriend, cat and housemate. She writes code for a living and writes about cooking for fun.*

# NEW LEASE ON LIFE

WORDS BY NIKAELA MARIE PETERS & PHOTOGRAPH BY OLIVIA RAE JAMES

*What gives a house life? After the birth of her first child, one writer discovers how her home became a living, breathing fourth member of the family.*

Becoming a parent is difficult to talk and write about, not because the words are hard to find (though they are), but because when you find them, they feel too intimate to share. The smells and sounds and stirrings of the heart are individual and holy. There's a sense in which the universal experience is yours alone when the opposite is actually true. You hesitate to say anything at all, as if staying quiet better preserves the miracle.

When my son was born, my house became alive. I noticed it in the first week. The structure I'd come to accept as ordinary—an early-1920s middle-class home with a stone foundation, hardwood floors and limestone moldings in the porch—started acting extraordinarily. In the otherwise silent night, save for the sounds of a suckling newborn, I was sure I could hear the house breathing. The creaks and clanks turned to sighs and moans as my ears attuned to raw infant cries. The water in the pipes was lifeblood, quenching my nursing thirst, washing swaddling blankets and bathing the delicate babe. The old battleship furnace in the basement chugged along, a burning beating heart, thumping steam through galvanized-steel arteries and regulating the temperature of each room.

A pregnant polar bear stays awake in her den in order to keep her temperature high enough to give birth and then nurse her cubs. Like her, our house stayed warm—and awake—that first winter. I imagined the floorboards tracking our movements and the windows monitoring our breaths. They were drawing maps of our quotidian behavior, charting sleeping statistics, mealtimes, visitors. It could've all been sleep deprivation and cabin fever but, without question, I came to believe our house was in some way conscious. We were not three: We were four.

The architectural theorist Dr. Hélène Frichot believes in the idea of a living building with fluid boundaries: walls that change with the life inside them. Weather and people and time should affect buildings for the better. Space stretches to accommodate life. It adapts to humans instead of the contrary.

In 29 years, I have called six places home—seven, if I distinguish between our house before and after my son was born. Of these, I have favorites. I liked my brightly painted first apartment with the rusty bath and windowless kitchen. I liked my lonely mat on the floor with the spiders and geckos in the attic in northern Thailand. And I like my messy, living house now: one where I'm awake nights and tired days, where things are ad hoc and provisional. Home and house are not one and the same.

I say that having a baby brought my house to life. And by coming to life, it turned from a structure into an environment, a possession into an ecosystem. A house is a geographic location, a street address. A home is where, and with whom, life happens. In my first apartment, *home* was my roommate and a third-story-window view. In Thailand, *home* was a pillow and a pile of letters. Now, *home* is a sweet 10-month-old and the words I can hear his dad reading to him in the other room: "A comb and a brush and a bowl full of mush..." That miracle I hesitate to describe. ○ ○ ○

*Nikaela Marie Peters lives in Winnipeg, Canada. She is currently completing graduate studies in theology.*

*Photograph of Colin, Lauren and Rex Pinegar taken in Charleston, South Carolina.*

# HOW TO BE NEIGHBORLY: THE HOUSEMATES EDITION

WORDS BY GEORGIA FRANCES KING & ILLUSTRATIONS BY SARAH BURWASH

*How do you live in a group house and still maintain good relationships with all of your housemates? Try our room-by-room guide to keeping a shared house clean, the vibe easygoing and the toilet paper well stocked.*

**KITCHEN** If there's one rule you should abide by for a harmonious household, it's this: Do not eat someone else's peanut butter, ever. Ever. Passive-aggressive food labeling is hardly a solution either. Sure, that may have been your resolution in the college kitchen, but aren't we all adults now with the memory spans and morals to remember if you have ownership over that pickle jar or not? Rather than be caught red-handed with a fist full of stolen strawberries, simply ask if you need to borrow some buttermilk or have an urgent salami craving that needs immediate addressing. Many households also contain a multitude of eating preferences and food allergies, from vegan warriors to those flirting with imaginary wheat intolerances. To organize the kitchen easily to all requests, allot each housemate a shelf in the refrigerator and pantry: this way someone's tahini doesn't have to buddy up with the raw steak. Feuds over chores and late bills can be avoided by sticking a whiteboard on the fridge to allocate and tick off duties. Keep two jars above the freezer: one for bill payments and one for a household kitty. Ask each home member to put an additional weekly five bucks in the latter for mutual cleaning supplies, toilet paper, plastic wrap and other necessary goods. Dishwashing detergent wars, be gone!

**LAUNDRY** For washer-less households, the weekly dirty hamper haul can be made more enjoyable in twos. Chatting over spin cycles gives you something to do aside from turning yourself cross-eyed watching the dryer tumble. If you're lucky enough to have a washer-dryer combo tucked away somewhere, there are guidelines to follow. Don't leave your damp towels gathering mildew at the bottom of the machine for days, offer to save energy by merging half-full baskets with other household members' items (just keep the reds and whites in different time zones), and don't turn your living room into a whitewashed tepee

by air-drying all of your sheets simultaneously. Instead, whenever the weather is nice outside, set up a rope between two trees and dry your linens that way. (This method has the added advantage of doubling as an outdoor cinema screen.) And a super-simple tip for waiting longer between loads? Just buy more underwear: that way your dresser will stay stocked with clean delicates and you can launder when you want to, not when you need to. Both your water bill and the environment will thank you for it.

**DINING ROOM** Even though you may feel like you see traces of your fellow dwellers on a daily basis (their cakes temptingly cooling on the counter, their mud tracked in through the front hall, their bobby pins sitting on the sink), coming together for regular meals really sets the mood for a successful shared house. Either organize a potluck or take turns cooking a full banquet for your housemates, three courses and all. Make sure to ask in advance before using housemates' special crockery, as you never know which vestibule could potentially be a family heirloom or contain Aunt Ida's dusty remains. After dining, clear the plates and try to wash them that night, as the whole I'll-do-it-tomorrow mantra often leads to dirty dishes teetering in Pisa-style piles. And remember the saying: "He who doth cooks shalt not have to spend 20 minutes forearm-deep in suds."

**BEDROOM** Where you lay your head each night may be your own private space, but that doesn't mean your incense and late-night wooing attempts don't find their way under the door, wafting into the nasal and aural passages of the household. Generally assume that if you can hear your wall-mate's misguided electric guitar aspirations, then he likely knows about your affinity for musical theater soundtracks. So be respectful and keep noise down to a minimum after hours or plug in a pair of headphones and restrain sing-alongs. When you're not in your room, close the door so people don't have to see your floor-bound clothing organizing system. Finally, when it comes to the domain of others' sanctuaries, always knock before entering and people will learn that you expect the same.

**BATHROOM** Your sink shouldn't resemble a massacre at the hairdresser. Girls should unblock the drain after each shampoo and boys should learn to throw their facial hair trimmings in the trash can—not down the sink, which leaves your pipes clogged and coughing up toothpaste gunk. If you have more than a 2-1 ratio of housemates to bathrooms, organize a morning schedule for showers and teeth brushing to avoid cold water and colder shoulders. And ladies: Your male counterparts may have been versed in the birds and the bees in high school, but they can still get squirmy around "girlie things." Either school them in contemporary feminist principles (preferable) or, if they can't grow up and handle a little nature, place your delicates in a private space, but ask them to do the same for equality's sake. Sometimes living together is about a bit of take, but a lot of give. ○ ○ ○

# THE HOLIDAY HOUSE

WORDS BY LIZ CLAYTON & PHOTOGRAPH BY TIM ROBISON

*The vacation home is where memories are formed, nostalgia is nurtured and plenty of growing up happens. One writer remembers the time spent at her folks' not-quite-country home and the stories it still holds.*

Almost every winter, I spend time on the beach. Not in the snowbird sense, but in the walk-across-the-street-from-my-parents'-country-house sense, where the long quiet stretch of Indiana dunes means tall grass blanketed in snow, and still-white waves frozen in place with ice and sand.

It's hardly the country, but also hardly anything like the lakefront tower on the south side of Chicago where I was really raised, only 57 miles away. Like anywhere you've lived part-time, the house feels like a specter. It's not really home but it also is: Its reach, once limited to weekends and summers, is now where memories linger, maybe because time there always felt so fleeting.

Michigan City, Indiana (why not love a border town whose name appropriates what it's not?), once reigned as an accessible paradise of sorts, not just for disgruntled Illinoisan beach tourists but also for those on grand cross-country tours along US 12. This "city"—slightly famous for, variously, Sansabelt pants, American-crafted Bromwell flour mills and the boiler that now heats my Brooklyn brownstone—straddles both its linen postcard past and its failed '80s renaissance. Visit the Indiana Dunes National Lakeshore and see tall piles of sand! Stop in at the Washington Park Zoo—which had its heyday in the 1960s, it would seem—and watch the monkeys cavort on a tall metal tower trapped in a futuristic concrete pit. Wear your bathing costume down to Lake Michigan and admire the sailboats, the people in striped summer joie de vivre and the tiny Chicago skyline beyond the catwalk to the lighthouse. And before you leave, don't forget to visit the dead mall!

We inherited the house from an old but modern-minded retired couple: Their curious tastes always made it feel like they were still there, calmly calling the shots. They'd outfitted the beach house with velvet chairs, midcentury green-and-blue shag carpets and white cast-iron lawn furniture. And did I mention the entire window-walled, wood-paneled main floor came with electric drapes, still fully operational? What was this place, Vegas?

Although it was neither fancy nor falling apart, the house's identity was always in conflict. Was its linoleum-heavy self once more ostentatious? One day, elderly strangers wandered down the looping driveway and revealed that where the shed now stood was once a cabana shower, and that there used to be a tennis court over the top of what today is a cellar room beguilingly filled with four feet of sand.

In my youth, it was a neighborhood misfit: a summer home visited year round, a place where my dad read science journals while those who rented party houses across the street dispatched noisy guitar licks and funny-smelling smoke into the quietly hammocked yard each summer night.

In this way, the house stayed in a strange compartment of our brains and our lives. It felt far from the heart of town yet completely informed by its weirdness. Away from our everyday routines, it fixed in our memories differently over the passing days and decades, uncluttered by the baggage from school or jobs. In my mind or in real life sometime soon, I'll leave my keys and wallet behind and climb over the shifting sandy hill to beachgoers and campfire remnants or simply no one. There, I'll look out at the linen-postcard panorama of a lighthouse and a life that's actually real. ○ ○ ○

*Liz Clayton is a writer and photographer based in Brooklyn. Her work has appeared in* Serious Eats, The Globe and Mail *and* The Yo La Tengo Gazette. *She recently released* Nice Coffee Time, *a book of photographs from cafés and kitchens around the world.*

# CALIFORNIA DREAMING

*A Venice Beach couple has found home in a 1975 modern box
made of simple materials such as concrete, wood and glass, just a short walk
from the ocean and the local bespoke shop they own. Hannah Henderson,
John Moore and their family share their shelter for the day.*

PHOTOGRAPHS BY CHRIS & SARAH RHOADS OF WE ARE THE RHOADS
STYLING BY LISA MOIR

**HOW DOES YOUR HOME REFLECT WHO YOU ARE?**

It's very much a California boy and desert girl home. John is very connected to the ocean, and I'm influenced by my mom, who is a midwife in Arizona. She always had a great respect for everything natural like plants, sun and fabrics. You can see that in our house.

**PLEASE DESCRIBE AN AVERAGE DAY IN YOUR HOME.**

We claim the weekends as our own: We try not to make plans so we can be free to do anything we want. John usually starts his day with a surf down the street while the kids and I laze around in bed. We like to be homebodies, make popcorn, watch movies, hang out, play records and take care of our plants. The kids make crafts and build forts.

**CAN YOU ELABORATE ON YOUR STYLE OF DECORATION?**

You can really feel the difference in things that are handmade or a vintage piece that has lived many lives over the years. There's love in things that were important to someone, and we have a lot of respect for that. We run a shop called General Store, so we're lucky to have great relationships with some amazing California craftspeople and artisans. They're a constant inspiration to us. There's also a good amount of vintage from local flea markets and the signs of a healthy Etsy obsession.

**DO YOU HAVE ANY ADVICE FOR HOW TO APPROACH INTERIOR DECORATING?**

Put care into the items you choose to bring into your home, and think about who made them. Rugs and plants are the simplest things you can use to transform a space. And throwing a great textile over a sad chair or table can give you extra years of enjoyment. Don't decorate to please anyone but yourself: It's your sanctuary.

**HOW DO YOU PREPARE WHEN ENTERTAINING IN YOUR HOME?**

We usually entertain on a last-second basis: We like our guests to come over spontaneously. We keep it very casual, but good food and drinks are necessary! We eat sitting on pillows on the floor with red wine and cartoons playing in the background.

**WHAT CHALLENGES HAS YOUR HOUSE PRESENTED YOU WITH?**

A small house means there's nowhere to hide from the kiddos and nowhere for them to hide from the grown-ups. It's taught us to establish our boundaries and learn to be respectful when people need space, alone time or quiet. The kids get the same respect as the grown-ups. It's pretty small but well-designed: There's enough space for everything we need and no space for anything more than that.

**HOW DO YOUR CHILDREN INTERACT WITH YOUR HOME?**

Very simple: They destroy it and we clean it up!

**WHAT WILL YOUR PREVAILING MEMORY OF THIS HOUSE BE?**

John bought it about a month before we met and we've been here for 12 years now! It's evolved constantly and matured with us. This is where we started our family. Our kids are growing up here, but John and I grew up here in a sense too. When I moved in, we were kids. A lot of changes happen in a decade of your youth, and all of those changes are wrapped up in this house. ○ ○ ○

# THE CONCEPT OF HOME

*From one end of life to the other, our feelings about home change. We ask some writers around the world to tell us what home means to them.*

**JORDAN HERNANDEZ: THE CHILDHOOD DWELLER** *Home* is one of the first words we learn as a child. It falls from our mouths and rolls off the tongue the way *mom* and *dad* do, providing a sense of where we belong. I still remember my first home: the white shutters, the slanted, creaky hallway and the light blue carpet. I remember blowing out birthday candles and seeing snow from the front windows for the first time. It was the only place I recognized as a haven strong enough to collect my childhood. When we moved, I cried in the back of our van as the bricks that laid the foundation to all my memories became a small speck in the rearview mirror. Then there's the defining moment when you return to an old house that you once knew so well and suddenly feel like a stranger. The cracks and crevices that once held your secrets no longer recognize your voice. You'll never stop mourning the loss of a first home but rather grow more resilient each time you move. Allow yourself sentimental feelings when you leave a piece of yourself behind somewhere, and look forward to blowing out more candles in a new place.

**AUSTIN SAILSBURY: THE NESTER** We started out like newlyweds often do: deep in love, low on cash and living with mismatched furniture. But then we moved to Scandinavia and discovered a whole new way of nesting. Day by day, a little at a time, we've made a home for ourselves. Here are the best lessons we've learned so far: 750 square feet (70 square meters) are, in fact, enough room for man and wife to live, work and dream together in harmony. Having less stuff is the best way to fight against clutter. An artful light can become a surrogate sun during the dark season. Only homemade furniture will ever properly fit the crooked walls and sloping floors of a stubborn old apartment. A good kettle and a faithful oven are worthy investments for their work is never done. You can't put a price on dependable neighbors or a view of the sea. And lastly, we've learned to put candles in the windows like tiny flickering lighthouses so that friends and loved ones will always be safely guided home.

**MOLLY YEH: THE FARMER** Our day begins with eggs from a nearby coop. My farmer leaves for his long harvest hours and my day of homey solitude brings a cake flavored with rosemary from the farmstead garden. My previous life in New York wasn't for this solitude or private cake: There was always somewhere to be, something new to do. My apartment wasn't my home—the city was my home. The park was my living room complete with boats and a castle. My apartment was a temporary space, a sleeping place. In North Dakota, my new town offers what half a New York block would. With air to breathe and permission to be still with the land, I can finally love my very own space. Just past dark, when my farmer comes in, he carries elk gifted by Tom from down the road. We prepare it for our supper and enjoy it at the table that we built. Later, the silence and the stars tuck us to sleep.

**LOUISA THOMSEN BRITS: THE EVERYWHERER** Home is about presence, not property. Thoughts of home follow the contours of landscape and memory, but the shape of home shifts as I grow less attached to stuff and can live closer to the heart of things. Home is a clearing in a patch of woodland, the curve of a hill, the pulse of life on a dance floor, a shared blanket, birch trees, backyard fires, a strip of beach, dusk, a place to plant things. Home is a lit lantern, slow mornings, spooning, the smell of coffee and wind-dried washing, the dust and heat of Africa, silence, bare feet, everyday rituals, a notebook, a dark field, a small hand in mine. Home is our wooden table with its burn and pen marks, cup rings and scratches, and our huge bed of mattresses pushed together on the floor. Home is wherever we discover we belong: to a place, to another or to a passing moment. Home is honesty, acceptance and relatedness: complicity, community and connection wherever we are.

**MIKE PERRY: THE PARENTAL RESIDER** Living with your parents can be a strange, bittersweet thing. I moved back in right after college to get my life in order and then set out on my own. It was a nice change of pace from the school life: Laundry was getting done by someone else and dinner was real food, not just microwave noodles or yesterday's pizza. I figured I'd stay a few months, but those months became a few years. I moved out again for a year, trying to carve out a life in another country. Unfortunately things there didn't quite pan out and I found myself back home, again. As I find myself approaching 30 in a struggling economy, it can be difficult and stressful at times—for everyone. But, as with everything, you take the bad with the good, and I'm lucky to have such supportive parents who are happy to have their son still home.

**SHELBY GILL: THE MOBILE HOMER** For me, home is ever-changing, not one static place. It doesn't have to be brick and mortar: Sometimes home just is. Sometimes home is sitting at the counter of my parent's kitchen and listening to my mother sing Johnny Cash songs while she makes gazpacho; I've never liked gazpacho, but she does, and that makes me happy. So maybe home is the fact that, in that brief moment, she's happy too. Sometimes home is the third booth back in a small café on Gregg Street, squeezed somewhere behind the woman who plays the mandolin on the front patio and the man who reads the local paper over a double Americano. So maybe home is that feeling of familiarity. Sometimes home is the second chapter of a really good book, where you're just far enough to be familiar, but haven't been reading long enough to feel stagnant. So maybe home is just that comfortable place between beginnings and ends. No matter which it is, home is the place that never seems to be stationary. It changes, and so do I.

**REBECCA PARKER PAYNE: THE HOMEOWNER** The story of my husband and I is not just about me, him or us, but a story of place. It's a story of how we married, wrapped warmly in the arms of our community, and bought this tiny house not unlike a small brick box for us to make livable and loved. Ours is a story of believing that buying a house is more than a mortgage and lawn care: It's understanding that making a home is a responsibility to the walls you live in, the ground you walk on and all the people that will tread here. There's no escaping this responsibility for us. Ours is a story now intertwined with this place—inseparable, really. Ours is a story that will unfold and grow here. This is the place of our home and the place of our lives, and I'm grateful for it. ○ ○ ○

# INSIDE JOB

PHOTOGRAPHS BY LUISA BRIMBLE

*What's the secret to working from home successfully?*
*We asked some seasoned home-based workers for ideas on getting the job done.*

## HANNAH FERRARA

JEWELRY DESIGNER
ASHEVILLE, NORTH CAROLINA

—

### WORKSPACE

I share a full studio workshop with my husband in a space located off the front part of our home. It's nice because we can shut the door to this area and my unfinished work isn't staring me in the face.

### PROS

When we first moved in, we chose this area for the studio as it gets the best natural light. It filters through a 100-year-old oak tree. I love watching that tree and its shadows change with the seasons.

### CONS

In winter's cold months you want to stay in bed just a few minutes more, or in the summer you want to skip work altogether and spend every waking moment outdoors.

### TIPS

I'm an avid list maker, so setting daily goals can really help with making sure you are making a dent in your workload, and the feeling of checking them off is unmatched.

## LIZ CLAYTON

WRITER/PHOTOGRAPHER
BROOKLYN, NEW YORK

—

### WORKSPACE

I have a home office with a real ergonomic chair and everything, but I would say 80 percent of work takes place at the kitchen table. And occasionally the couch.

### CONS

Constant distraction by mundane household tasks that are otherwise repulsive, unless I'm on deadline. Cat trying to sleep on hands while typing.

### PROS

You can get a snack whenever.

### TIPS

The only thing that works reliably for me is to schedule enough tasks or appointments, or create enough external pressure somehow, that deadlines force themselves into place. I find that as bad as distractions are, they can push you to do more.

## ALEX MITCHELL

CURATOR/ARTIST
LYON, FRANCE

—

### WORKSPACE

I work from a secluded studio in a dark corner of our apartment. Or any stable surface with an adjacent power supply.

### TIPS

The line between work and play is going to get blurry, but don't stress. Just roll with it. Eventually there will be no distinction between the two at all. And why should there be? What's the point of living if you're not achieving things, and what's the point of achieving things if it isn't fun?

### CONS

My gallery is back in Australia, so as far as curators go I'm essentially a brain in a jar. The toughest part was putting together a team who could be my arms, legs and, should the need arise, various other appendages. I got lucky: My team is great.

### PROS

Right now I'm sitting at my desk in my underwear.

### SARA PADGETT HEATHCOTT

MUSIC LABEL OWNER
PORTLAND, OREGON

—

**WORKSPACE**

My workspace exploded out of a
dedicated office almost as soon as I set up
my desk. I'll jump and run to my couch
at any given moment or hop down to
the basement where we store records and
pack mail orders.

**PROS/CONS**

The toughest part about working at
home is also its most magical aspect:
You're always surrounded by what you
make. At any given moment I'm staring
down a stack of boxes taller than me that
don't just contain records—they contain
years of dreaming and devotion, a ton of
sweat, the art of my best friends and the
winding road ahead.

**TIPS**

No checking your email in bed. When
you love what you do—when it defines
you and your community—motivation
and productivity are never a problem.
What is a problem: remembering to
stop. While it does enable me to go all
superhuman and grow extra arms and
eyes, constantly working doesn't always
stoke the fire that started it all in
the first place.

### MONICA LOCASCIO

CREATIVE CONSULTANT
NEW YORK, NEW YORK

—

**WORKSPACE**

It's a home office built into my beautiful studio
apartment: a standing desk, a printer/scanner,
lots of natural light coming through two big
eastern-facing windows, plants, a tea kettle and
a comfortable couch for thinking.

**PROS**

My kitchen and naptime!

**CONS**

Staying focused on the task at hand. There's
always a plant to repot, a cabinet to organize
or a baby blanket to finish.

**TIPS**

Taking a real lunch break is essential. I make
a beautiful fresh meal and take my time
eating, ideally followed with a walk outside
to get some fresh air. Also, pay attention to
your mood—if you're restless or unfocused,
don't force it. Take advantage of your
situation and get out for some inspiration.

### KAI BRACH

PUBLISHER/DESIGNER
MELBOURNE, AUSTRALIA

—

**WORKSPACE**

Our small apartment has a second little
bedroom where I work. As hard as it is, it's
important to be able to close that door at the
end of the day and keep things separate.

**TIPS**

I tend to divide my time into
smaller chunks by scheduling doctor
appointments, grocery shopping and
exercise throughout the day. It's too easy
to get stuck behind a screen for 10 hours
without leaving the house once.

**CONS**

I miss having colleagues that I can talk to
and bounce ideas off of. As much as water-
cooler conversations are a productivity
killer, they do make your work more fun.

**PROS**

While many of my friends are sitting in
their cars battling road rage or are cramped
into overcrowded, smelly trains running
late for work, I brew my first cup of coffee
and soak up the morning serenity of being
home alone. ○ ○ ○

# THE CHEF'S KITCHEN

*Three London chefs—Fergus Henderson, Florence Knight
and Skye Gyngell—invite us over for tea, show us around
their homes and give us some simple recipes they make away
from the hustle and bustle of a commercial kitchen.*

# FERGUS HENDERSON

INTERVIEW BY GAIL O'HARA & PHOTOGRAPH BY INDIA HOBSON

Fergus Henderson is the founder of the St. John restaurants and author of *Nose to Tail Eating: A Kind of British Cooking* (titled *The Whole Beast* in the US), which highlights his simple food philosophy. We caught up with Fergus to see how he lives and eats at home.

AS THE SON OF TWO ARCHITECTS, WHAT KIND OF MEMORIES DO YOU HAVE OF YOUR CHILDHOOD HOME?

When I was growing up, I remember white walls and lots of Aalto stools. My mum is a great cook and my dad was a big eater. Everything changed with the arrival of Marcella Hazan's *Classic Italian Cookbook*. After this landed, there was no looking back.

HOW LONG HAVE YOU BEEN IN YOUR CURRENT HOME?

My parents designed this house. We've been living here for 20 years. It seems like a certain chaos goes with the family territory. Unfortunately, we have managed to give our house a very well-lived-in look. When I see other people's homes, I'm constantly impressed by the lack of chaos: Lightbulbs work, oven doors aren't falling off, pictures are framed and hanging on the wall rather than leaning in random piles, all the plumbing is working. How do they do it? Hats off to them.

CAN YOU TELL US A LITTLE MORE ABOUT THE HISTORY OF THE HOUSE YOU LIVE IN?

In Victorian times, they attempted to improve Seven Dials, the area where we live, as it had become a terrible area of carousing, fighting, whores and drinking. Charles Dickens refused to go to the place. Town houses were built that were rapidly converted into banana warehouses. The fighting stopped, so did the drinking and the women, and the town houses were turned into flats.

WHAT KIND OF PANTRY STAPLES, GADGETS AND COOKWARE COULD YOU NOT FUNCTION WITHOUT?

Personally, I couldn't function without a corkscrew and a wooden spoon. We've amassed a huge collection of cooking implements but those two remain the most useful. And it's incredible: Whenever you look into the recesses of the fridge there's always a jar of capers. It's very reassuring.

DO YOU AND YOUR FAMILY HAVE ANY RITUALS FOR EVERYDAY MEALS AT HOME?

Eating and drinking wine is ritual enough, but always lay a table. It's vital to have this rigor.

HOW DID HAVING A FAMILY CHANGE YOUR CONCEPT OF HOME?

Fitting in all the hurrumphing teenagers somewhere! Kids give meaning to a home.

WILL YOU LIVE IN THIS HOME FOREVER?

No! Change is good, and we are all also getting bigger! We need more space and a garden.

WHAT DO YOU MAKE WHEN YOU ENTERTAIN FOR FRIENDS AND FAMILY AT HOME?

I make Tomato Pasta (see the recipe on the following spread), or Margot roasts a grand chicken, but this can depend on the vibrations.

HOW DO YOU COOK DIFFERENTLY AT HOME THAN YOU DO IN A COMMERCIAL KITCHEN?

Fundamentally, we never cook pastas at the restaurant. Geography also comes into it: The only decent shop near our home is an Italian deli. For numerous reasons, things taste different in restaurants than at home, thank goodness!

# TOMATO PASTA

RECIPE BY FERGUS HENDERSON & PHOTOGRAPH BY GENTL & HYERS

Fergus says: "This is a dish that represents absolute comfort. It's something that you never tire of, a dish with supernatural healing powers that seems to cure everything from teenage angst to life in general. Where we live, the only good shop is a small Italian delicatessen. All of the other shops are representatives of the evil empires: the supermarkets! So our diet is led by the Italian goodies, and the most recurring dish is this tomato pasta."

*1 (16-ounce/450-gram) package of dried spaghetti*

*2 (28-ounce/790-gram) cans plum tomatoes*

*2 red onions, peeled and sliced*

*4 cloves of garlic, peeled and sliced*

*Extra-virgin olive oil*

*Sea salt*

*Freshly ground black pepper*

*Parmesan cheese, for serving*

METHOD In a large saucepan, warm a healthy splash of oil over medium-high heat. Fry off the onion and garlic until they soften, about 5 minutes, then add tomatoes, salt and pepper. Simmer over medium-low heat as long as you can, until the sauce has thickened and the tomatoes have broken down.

Bring liberally salted water to boil in a large pot. Cook the spaghetti and drain.

Mix with the sauce and serve with freshly grated Parmesan. ○ ○ ○

*Serves 4*

# FLORENCE KNIGHT

INTERVIEW BY GEORGIA FRANCES KING & PHOTOGRAPH BY INDIA HOBSON

Florence Knight is the head chef at Polpetto, author of a recent cookbook titled *One: A Cook and Her Cupboard* and a girl about town. We ask her about what kind of grub she enjoys at home, how she likes living there and what pantry items she can't live without.

### AFTER A DAY IN THE RESTAURANT, DO YOU STILL COOK DECADENTLY OR PLAINLY FOR YOURSELF?

I'm a grazer who's committed to the best quality ingredients I can get my hands on. Meals at home usually consist of things I've collected from farmers markets with seasonal vegetables, relatively locally smoked salmon and meat from my local butcher. After a day of tasting such a wide variety of dishes, I just want to eat simple food that keeps the wolf from the door, like hot buttered toast, fennel tea and yogurt.

### WHAT STAPLES DO YOU ALWAYS KEEP ON HAND IN YOUR FRIDGE AND PANTRY FOR QUICK POSTWORK DISHES?

The fridge always has some charcuterie as well as some hard cheese such as Parmesan and Coolea that doesn't go off easily. My hours are pretty erratic once I'm in full swing with the restaurant, so it's best not to have anything that deteriorates too quickly. Homemade pickles and chutneys are among the jars. We also always keep eggs, lentils, rice and fresh herbs on hand.

### HOW CAN THE AVERAGE HOME COOK MAKE THEIR EVENING MEAL FEEL MORE RESTAURANT QUALITY?

Choosing seasonal ingredients is crucial: They'll taste better and be easily available, whether it's white currants, bobby beans, sloe berries, quinces, acorns, cocoa beans or nettles. I recommend stocking the kitchen with a few key ingredients. These are the building blocks, a kind of backbone to any dish: Olive oil, salt, honey, chocolate, vinegar, flour, eggs, mustard, nuts, unwaxed lemons and lots of fresh herbs are what make simple food shine.

### DO YOU HAVE A ROUTINE YOU FOLLOW BEFORE OR AFTER WORK?

I'm very spoiled. My husband makes me breakfast that usually consists of espresso, freshly squeezed juice, a big bowl of porridge with fresh fruit and a slice of toast. It's something of a family tradition. And I can never leave the house without making the bed.

### HOW LONG HAVE YOU BEEN IN YOUR CURRENT HOUSE?

I'm at the end of the restoration of a Georgian house in the middle of Soho in central London. It was built in 1734 and was a brothel for at least 150 years. The Beatles recorded their first few albums a few doors down, including "Hey Jude," and Marianne Faithfull used to busk here when she was down on her luck. Most of the original features had been ripped out or covered over so we've spent a great deal of time restoring floors, fireplaces, walls, staircases and ceilings. Many of our belongings have traveled back with us from our trips to Paris, San Sebastián and Williamsburg flea markets. Hurtling down the platform for the Eurostar laden with two enormous mottled mirrors is a memory that will stay with me.

### WHO ELSE LIVES IN YOUR HOME?

I live with my husband and two dogs called Guinevere and Edna. They make my home the place I want to be.

### WHAT AREA OF THE HOME DO YOU SPEND THE MOST TIME IN AND WHY?

As with most homes, the kitchen is the room that everyone gravitates to. The first piece of furniture my husband and I bought together was our beautiful oak kitchen table. It must be something to do with sitting around the primordial fire, sharing, being together and eating together.

# SOFT-BOILED EGGS & BUTTERED SOLDIERS

RECIPE BY FLORENCE KNIGHT & PHOTOGRAPH BY GENTL & HYERS

**F**lorence says: "I have many happy memories of tapping the top of my egg with a spoon and dipping soldiers [toast cut into strips and lined up like soldiers at attention] into runny amber yolks. Boiling eggs may seem simple but there are a lot of factors: Always use the freshest eggs at room temperature, note that the ratio of water to eggs will alter the cooking time, and the best results will come from using a pot that comfortably houses a couple of eggs with about 1 inch of water above their heads."

### SOFT-BOILED EGGS

*2 large free-range eggs, at room temperature*

**METHOD** Place the eggs in a small heavy-bottomed saucepan and fill with enough cold water to cover by 1 inch/2.5 centimeters. Bring to a boil over high heat. Once boiling, reduce heat to a gentle simmer and cook for 2 1/2 minutes for soft, runny yolks. (You'll need a runny yolk to dip your soldiers into, but if you prefer a "set egg" then simmer for 4 minutes, or 6 for hard-boiled.)

### SOLDIERS WITH SAGE & CHILI BUTTER

*2 tablespoons (30 grams) salted butter,*
*at room temperature*

*5 sage leaves, torn*

*A generous pinch of dried chili flakes*

*1 thick slice of bread*
*(makes 6 soldiers)*

**METHOD** Pound the sage in a mortar and pestle (alternatively, pound them in a small bowl with the back of a wooden spoon) until coarse and shredded. Add the chili and pound to combine. Place the butter in a small bowl and stir in the sage and chili mixture.

Toast the bread, then spread one side with the chili butter. Cut into soldiers, ready to dip into the runny yolks.

### SOLDIERS WITH BURNT BUTTER, ROSEMARY AND PARMESAN

*4 sprigs of rosemary, leaves roughly chopped*

*1 tablespoon (3 grams) Parmesan*

*A generous pinch of salt*

*4 tablespoons (60 grams) butter*

*1 thick slice of bread*
*(makes 6 soldiers)*

**METHOD** Combine the rosemary, Parmesan and salt on a small baking tray.

Melt the butter in a medium skillet over medium heat, and cut the toast into soldiers. Once it begins to foam, place the dippable-size soldiers in the skillet. The kitchen will be filled with the smell of biscuits and the bread will turn a golden brown. Spoon the foaming butter over the bread and turn them after 1 minute to get an even dark golden brown on each side.

Once the soldiers are evenly browned and crisp, remove the bread with a slotted spoon and roll them over the Parmesan mixture on the tray until all are evenly coated. ○ ○ ○

*Serves 1*

# SKYE GYNGELL

INTERVIEW BY GEORGIA FRANCES KING & PHOTOGRAPH BY INDIA HOBSON

Acclaimed Australian chef Skye Gyngell is a cookbook author and food writer (and a former food editor at *British Vogue*) who won praise for her cooking at Petersham Nurseries Café and the French House in London. She invites us into her home to see how she cooks for herself and her family.

**PLEASE TELL US ABOUT THE DISHES YOU OFTEN MAKE AT HOME.**

We eat fairly simply at home. I love pulses and grains so I might cook a big pot of farro, which I lace with grassy, verdant extra-virgin olive oil, a little red wine vinegar and plenty of herbs. This pot sustains us for a day or two and we may add a little grilled fish or some green vegetables, but not much more than that during the week.

**WHAT STAPLES DO YOU ALWAYS KEEP ON HAND IN YOUR FRIDGE AND PANTRY?**

We always have good bread—we make ryes and sourdoughs at work and I always make sure there's a loaf or two extra to take home—some good unsalted butter, extra-virgin olive oil, red wine vinegar, sheep's milk yogurt, a hunk of aged Parmesan, whatever vegetables or fruit are in season, eggs (because if there's nothing else at all in the fridge, you can make a meal if you have eggs) and I'm never without a bowl of lemons on the kitchen table. My pantry is full of dried pulses and grains, tins of Ortiz anchovies and dried red chilies.

**WHAT KIND OF GADGETS AND COOKWARE COULD YOU NOT FUNCTION WITHOUT?**

I'm not great with gadgets: I feel most comfortable using my hands. I love my mortar and pestle, my old Bialetti coffeemaker and I enjoy collecting beautiful glasses.

**HOW CAN THE AVERAGE HOME COOK MAKE THEIR EVENING MEAL FEEL MORE RESTAURANT QUALITY?**

The lovely thing about home cooking is just that it's food cooked by real people at home. I have no desire to make home cooking like restaurant cooking. The difference should be celebrated.

**HOW DOES YOUR HOME REFLECT YOU?**

A lot of my life is spent in quite stressful, small spaces, so I love silence and solitude and really need it to reenergize myself. My garden is really important to me: It's full of herbs and vegetables such as tomatoes and rhubarb in the summer months, and it has the loveliest cherry tree that I rescued from the pavement outside our house where it had been abandoned. In the winter months I often retreat to my bedroom quite early. I read there or write menus—it's a room where I find it easy to think.

**WHAT HAVE YOU DONE WITH YOUR OWN HOUSE TO MAKE IT FEEL LIKE HOME?**

I've lived in this house for six years. It's a little cottage in Shepherd's Bush that was very run-down when I bought it: There was no central heating and it still had an outside loo. We really had to start from scratch to make it habitable and everything was done on a shoestring. My mother is an artist so it's filled with lots of her paintings. I miss Australia a lot, especially during the cold winter months, so the house is full of lots of color and things that remind me of warmer climates. We also have a dog called Luna, who is infuriatingly high-strung and causes havoc to my peace of mind. I have a dream that one day when the children are gone and I've made my fortune, I will have a really perfect, glamorous, tidy flat somewhere full of beautiful, impractical furniture. But I'm not sure it will ever happen or really make me happy.

# CHICKPEA AND CHARD SOUP

## RECIPE BY SKYE GYNGELL & PHOTOGRAPH BY GENTL & HYERS

S kye says: "More a meal than a soup, this is all I need to eat to pep me up at lunchtime during the week. Finished with a good splash of grassy, peppery extra-virgin olive oil, it is truly lovely."

---

*1 1/4 cups (300 grams) dried chickpeas, soaked overnight (see note)*

*3 tablespoons (45 milliliters) extra-virgin olive oil, plus extra for serving*

*Juice of 1/2 a lemon*

*2 dried red chilies*

*5 garlic cloves, peeled and smashed with the back of a knife*

*3 rosemary sprigs*

*2 (12-ounce/260-gram) cans good-quality peeled plum tomatoes*

*Sea salt and freshly ground black pepper*

*1 quart (1 liter) good-quality chicken stock (water or vegetable broth will also work)*

*About 6 stalks (10 ounces/300 grams) Swiss chard*

*2 slices of day-old, chewy, peasant-style bread, crusts removed*

*3 to 3 3/4 ounces (90 to 100 grams) Parmesan, freshly grated*

---

METHOD Drain the chickpeas, rinse and place in a large heavy pan. Cover generously with cold water, but don't season. Bring to a boil over medium heat, then turn down the heat. Simmer gently for 1 1/2 hours, or until the chickpeas are soft, skimming away any scum from the surface every now and then. Drain and dress with 1 tablespoon/15 milliliters olive oil and the lemon juice.

While the chickpeas are cooking, warm 2 tablespoons/30 milliliters olive oil in a separate pan over medium heat. Crumble in the chilies and add the garlic and rosemary. Cook for a minute or so to release the flavors, then add the tomatoes and stir well to break them up, adding a good pinch of salt. Cover and cook for 20 minutes, then pour in the stock and cook for another 10 minutes. Finally, add the cooked chickpeas and simmer gently for 40 minutes. Remove the rosemary sprigs.

Toward the end of the cooking time, prepare the chard. Wash and pat dry, then strip the leaves from the pale central stalk using a small sharp knife and set aside. Trim the stalks and cut into 1/2-inch (1.3-centimeter) chunks. Add these to a pan of well-salted boiling water and cook for 2 minutes, then add the soft green outer leaves and cook for another minute. Drain.

Break the bread into small pieces and stir into the soup along with 3 ounces/90 grams of Parmesan, turning the heat to low. Add the chard and a drizzle of olive oil. The soup should be deeply flavorful and thick. Add a little more Parmesan and/or olive oil if needed. Ladle into warm soup bowls and serve.

*Note:* If presoaking beans is beyond your usual level of organization (like me), there is an alternative. Rinse the beans, place them in a pan and cover with cold water, then bring to a boil. Drain, return to the pan and cover a second time with cold water, then cook as if the beans have been presoaked. ○ ○ ○

*Serves 4*

*This recipe is from the cookbook* My Favorite Ingredients *(Ten Speed Press) by Skye Gyngell.*

# THE KINFOLK HOME TOURS

In this special section of *Kinfolk,* we go beyond the welcome mats of a dozen houses from around the world. These home dwellers speak six different languages, come from four continents and represent all kinds of interpretations of the word *family*. Some of our subjects have pooled their friends' talents to construct a shiny new urban home from the blueprints up, while others are the seventh generation to live in a countryside cottage first occupied by their great-great-great-great-grandparents. Regardless of where these diverse structures are located or how they're decorated, these spaces are bound to inspire you and offer variations on the many ways you can live within your own space. Fill your environment with ideas, color it with personal history and paint it whatever color you please: Make it your home.

# THE SELF-MADE MODERNIST

*Suginami, Tokyo, Japan*

**RESIDENTS** Mariko Hirasawa and her husband Kohei

**OCCUPATIONS** Mariko: illustrator. Kohei: music label representative

**TYPE OF HOUSE** Modern Japanese home

**YEAR BUILT** 2013

---

Although her compact Tokyo house has a modern facade, Mariko has made a concerted effort to use natural materials in the building process, referencing her nation's past and preparing it for the future. "I'm looking forward to five or ten years from now. When it comes to trees, plaster and iron, time is not the enemy: It works to our advantage instead," she says. Just as the materials lend themselves to an eternity of enjoyment, she has kept her home personal and current by bringing together objects from people around her. She asked her friends to contribute various parts of the project, turning it into "a home built with everyone's love." The entire blueprint was designed by one of her dear friends from college, and the kitchen, bathroom and studio space were constructed by an architect she'd always admired. It was made using *shikkui* plaster, which is popular in traditional Japanese homes, to keep the summer humidity out, as well as a significant amount of wood to create a certain kind of softness. Like the average Tokyo home, it isn't exactly spacious, with rooms stacked on top of each other like Jenga blocks. Featuring an atelier at the top of their slanted staircase (where Mariko spends most of her day) and plenty of floor-to-ceiling windows, they take advantage of letting as much light as possible flood into their little space. Although her kitchen is similarly small, Mariko likes the way it allows her to have a conversation face to face while prepping a meal for visitors. "There's also a large tree you

can see from the windows, so it feels good to do kitchen chores," she says. "That feeling of comfort and ease must show in the food I cook as well." Just like anyone who's crafted their own home from the ground up, she has learned a thing or two about how to construct more than just walls: "Creating a home is about really knowing what makes you feel good. Would you like your room to have sunlight pour in or is it about having a place you can relax at night?" she says. "It's about knowing yourself and what your priorities are: That is what's important." ○

*Photographs by Hideaki Hamada &*
*Produced by Tina Minami Dhingra*

# THE CLASSIC SEVEN

*Jackson Heights, Queens, New York*

**RESIDENTS** Jesse James, Kostas Anagnopoulos (Gus) and their daughter Olympia
**OCCUPATIONS** Jesse: creative director. Kostas: poet/editor. Olympia: first-grader
**TYPE OF HOUSE** Prewar co-op apartment
**YEAR BUILT** 1924

Kostas and Jesse's apartment is what New York realtors call a "Classic Seven": a prewar apartment with a living room, dining room, kitchen and four bedrooms (plus three bathrooms, marble details, oak floors, a fireplace and griffin gargoyles guarding their front gate). If you're gasping at the thought of Manhattan folks living in anything larger than a bread box, their space comes with the neighborhood: Jackson Heights, Queens. This historic area boasts incredible buildings, rare garden spaces and is home to a diverse community that includes people hailing from Central America to Southeast Asia. Jesse says their aesthetic ends up being a "collective self-portrait," with three different people living in a space already imbued with so much

character. "Gus's essence can be found in a lot of the books and artwork, I suppose the mass of objects reflects my inclination to accumulate things and Olympia supplies the spontaneity, providing us with ever-changing, site-specific art installations using rocks, feathers and her many plastic animals." After moving in, their goal was to restore and simplify the previous owners' modern additions to "bring the bones back to the feeling of the 1920s." They restored the cupboards, redid the wiring, resurfaced the walls, refinished the floors, added some wainscoting, repaired the bathroom tiles, and that was only the start. Once they'd rebuilt the skeleton, they set about decorating with a mishmash of antiques from different eras. "Whatever the period, it's

always the patina that grabs us: The wear and tear that come with age adds emotion," Jesse says. "Car rides in the country take us twice as long as they should because we can't pass up a barn sale." The family cooks and shares dinner together most nights, and afterward Gus and Olympia lie with their ears to the floor and listen to their downstairs neighbor play the piano. Together they've created a private refuge within the walls of their home, ready to absorb some memories of its own. Using influences from your past and fusing them with your future—that's what good interior decorating requires. "Start by looking inward and defining what it is you want from a home. Think of the places and environments that are ingrained in your memory for the way that they make you feel," he says. "Those elements will stand the test of time." ○

*Photographs by Philip Ficks &*
*Prop Styling by Pam Morris*

# THE SURF SHACK

*Jan Juc, Victoria, Australia*

**RESIDENTS** Kirsty Davey and Simon Taylor, their daughter Mali, Mr. Brown the Labrador and Charlie the cat

**OCCUPATIONS** Kirsty: writer/stylist. Simon: agency owner

**TYPE OF HOUSE** Timber weatherboard

**YEAR BUILT** Circa 1950

---

Five years ago, Kirsty and Simon traded in their metropolitan Melbourne lives for a humble, quirky beach shack on the coastline two hours southwest of their previous home. The house features a huge nautical round window overlooking their kitchen and the rambling character of a cottage preserved by its former tenants. When they found it, they knew they'd scored an ideal spot just minutes from the surf. They slowly began to make it their own, first with knickknacks and then with their first child. Kirsty used to describe herself as a bowerbird of sorts, though now her decorating aesthetic and lifestyle fit a simpler mold. "We try to live minimally and sentimentally, surrounding ourselves with objects and talismans that are functional, beautiful and meaningful," she says. Their home is an amalgamation of items from local Australian designers and found objects from the side of the road, curated to fit together and create a rustic, cabin-like atmosphere. When the workday is over, it's not uncommon for the locals to join them for meals, backgammon, surf missions or just to share stories of wild parties and traveling musicians who have recorded music in their garage over the years. All year round, friends and family are invited to stay in the guest room—which doubles as Simon's surfboard quiver—and add to their rapidly collecting tales. ○

*Photographs by Kirsty Davey & Simon Taylor*

# THE NATURAL TRADITION

*Setagya, Tokyo, Japan*

**RESIDENTS** Yukiko Kuroda and her cat

**OCCUPATION** Kintsugi master (a traditional Japanese method of pottery repair)

**TYPE OF HOUSE** Single-story wooden building

**YEAR BUILT** 1946

---

From a glimpse it would appear that Yukiko's home is in Japan's wooded countryside, when it's really nestled between tall trees in a crowded inner Tokyo neighborhood. Although it was built postwar, it reflects the ancestral wisdom and cultural climate of a much older mode of traditional Japanese architecture. "I don't care so much for style," Yukiko says. "I want to stick with learning and taking on traditional Japanese methods by living in this home." The house is made mostly of a wood structure, tatami mat floors and shoji-paper dividing walls; she loves the soft light that filters through and the texture of nature beneath her feet. However, she doesn't understand why her ancestors thought paper was a smart construction material: "It's too easily broken by a finger or an enemy, like a samurai rushing through your house," she says, laughing. "Why didn't they choose a stronger material? It fascinates me." It's been custom to build a house designed to suit the height of summer since the 1300s when *Tsurezuregusa* (which translates to *Essays in Idleness,* a collection of thoughts by the monk Yoshida Kenkō that greatly influenced Japanese homemaking) was published. Most areas of her home do not have enough electricity to run simple things like air-conditioning, and Yukiko believes that we can live a comfortable life without such modern amenities. In her kitchen, microwaves and refrigerators aren't daily essentials. Instead, she pulls up cool water from the well on her property, uses ventilated bamboo

baskets to keep produce fresh, and pickles and ferments anything she can get her hands on, storing them in tall jars in her pantry. "No food, no life," she says. "I believe from the bottom of my heart that if I waste food, nature or any other thing, then I'll pay for it someday." This ties into her career as a master of *kintsugi*, a traditional Japanese way of fixing broken pottery natural lacquer called *urushi*, dirt, rice and powdered gold. Through adhering to these ancient ideals, she admits that she often fails when trying to remain true to her ethos but gets goose bumps every time she makes a small discovery through one of those failures. Because of this, her bond with her home is closer than most, forming a symbiotic teacher/student relationship. "I respect my home a lot and regard it as my mentor," she says. "I'm a pupil of my house." ○

*Photographs by Parker Fitzgerald &*
*Translation by Sakiko Setaka*

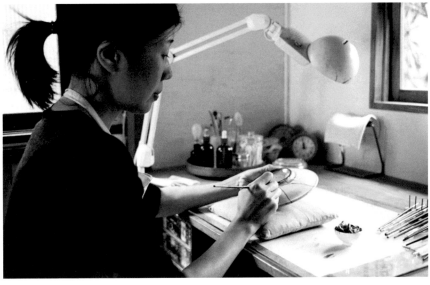

# THE FAMILY HEIRLOOM

*Roskilde, Zealand, Denmark*

**RESIDENTS** Agnete Dinesen and her dog
**OCCUPATION** Goldsmith
**TYPE OF HOUSE** Agricultural farmhouse
**YEAR BUILT** 1788

---

Not many people know where their family was living in the late 1700s and very few could say they still live in the same house where their great-great-great-great-grandfather once smoked his pipe. Agnete's relatives have been living in this quaint cottage in the Danish countryside for two and a half centuries. After growing up running around its wooden floorboards, she bought the house from her father in the '90s and has handled its maintenance (and organic vegetable garden) ever since. Over that time the structure hasn't changed all that much aside from a door or a wall here and there. Even the bric-a-brac has remained much the same: Generations of Dinesens have left their marks in the form of small tchotchkes or nicks in

the doorframes. When she needs a change in decor, she often heads to the attic and chooses another chair or side table left behind by her forefathers. Agnete is well-known as a traditional goldsmith, creating jewelry that's made using methods as old and authentic as the walls around her. Moss lines her home's slanted roof and the pathway is dotted with cobblestones that have seen the feet of hundreds of visitors over the eras. Agnete and her pup might be the only two still living here, but the walls creak stories of her heritage. It's truly a family home.  ○

*Photographs by Line T. Klein & Styling by Nathalie Schwer*

# THE WORK IN PROGRESS

*Strandboulevarden, Copenhagen, Denmark*

**RESIDENT** Niels Strøyer Christophersen

**OCCUPATION** Creative director

**TYPE OF HOUSE** Street-level apartment

**YEAR BUILT** 1905

---

After growing tired of the gentrifying coolness of his former neighborhood, Niels found this historically protected ground-floor apartment in a family-dominated seaside suburb, full of fresh air and joggers running around lakes. It has dark green window frames outlining a light gray exterior—a typical style for Copenhageners—though the inside proved a great canvas for taking it in a very personal direction. Although described by the realtor as a renovation project, the house showed potential. Fully aware it would need work, he set about morphing its under-loved innards into his personal zone. "I wanted people to see every room like it was a small adventure," he says. Wandering through the salvaged-material doorways around his home, visitors are often struck by the unfinished turquoise walls that are left bare with paintings leaning casually against the skirting boards. Niels got particularly lucky when it came to furniture: As the founder and creative director of his own design agency, he was lucky enough to have scored some collectible items along the way. "The contemporary pieces I have are very neutral in color, shape and materials, but they're distinguished and sophisticated," he says. "They blend in perfectly with my flea market brass pieces and auction-bought vintage safari chairs by Kaare Klint." He's discovered that slowly gathering your favorite pieces over time is essential to interior decorating. "Try to see it as a process: It's all right to wait for the right object to come

instead of going to a warehouse and buying all of your furniture. Create a nice little museum of beautiful memories," Niels says. Everything in his home is geared toward relaxing: He chose a bathtub over a shower, bookcases over a TV and treated his kitchen like a comfy couch. "It's more like a piece of furniture that's been transformed into a kitchen," he says. Niels prefers choosing high-quality natural products that are simple and give off a timeless appearance. He advocates going for quality and not compromising on price, and if all else fails, grab the paint. "When you don't have white walls, people will be impressed!" he says. "Kind of a joke, but also true." ○

*Photographs by Ditte Isager &*
*Styling by Nathalie Schwer*

# THE HATCH HOUSE

*Cape Cod, Massachusetts*

**ORIGINAL OWNERS** Ruth and Robert Hatch

**ARCHITECT** Jack Hall

**TYPE OF HOUSE** "The perfect modern primitive hut" —K. Michael Hays, Harvard architecture professor

**YEAR BUILT** 1962

In 1960, architect Jack Hall designed a summer cottage on the bay for Robert Hatch, an editor at *The Nation,* and his wife Ruth. According to Peter McMahon, author of *Cape Cod Modern: Midcentury Architecture and Community on the Outer Cape*, the rectangular structure was conceived as cubes in a grid matrix and was partly inspired by chicken coops. Framed by an exoskeleton of fir posts and beams, it divided its living space into three areas: a living room, a master suite and some guest rooms. The showpiece was its living and dining area that opened to a sea-facing deck via mosquito screens, Plexiglas sliders and wooden shutters with an emphasis on good light for reading. Exposed dark beams on painted plywood made the space feel both intimate and grand. The built-in couch seats were ideal for gazing at the bay. The artist Peter Watts, a family friend, remembers, "You could just be mesmerized sitting out on the porch. I always thought it was like living in a Turner painting." The Hatch family's lease ended in 2007, and now the house is currently owned by the National Park Service/Cape Cod National Seashore. Once a gathering spot for artists, thinkers and friends, including Noam Chomsky and Edmund Wilson, it is now completely restored and open for residencies, summer rentals and occasional tours.  ○

*Photographs by Anna Moller*

# THE MOUNTAIN CABIN

*Ainet de Besan, Lleida, Spain*

**RESIDENT** Mercè Piqué Camprubí

**OCCUPATION** Ceramist

**TYPE OF HOUSE** Stone and slate structure, wooden inside

**YEAR BUILT** Around 1750

Mercè was born in this cozy, rustic mountain cabin nestled amid breathtaking natural scenery in a town of 20 to 60 people; in fact, it's been in her family for a few generations. Some of her furniture came with the house and dates back to 1750. Made of thick stone walls and a form of adobe, the structure is typical of many mountain homes in the region. In the winter she spends a lot of time in a room that contains only a chimney and benches where she reads, reclines or is just hypnotized by the fire. As a ceramist who also works at a retirement home for the mentally ill, she sees her house as a personal refuge, a place where she feels calm, relaxed and alive. "When I come inside this house, it embraces me and everything melts together: memories of my childhood with my grandparents, naps and family meals. I've spent many special moments here with lifelong friends and my parents, and I'll never forget my grandfather's last summer here," she says. "I'm transported to a time that's slow but endearing and terribly heartfelt." Mercè explains that the house has a rich history: Strangely, it was dubbed "Casa de la Niña" (House of the Girl) because a woman lived there with her brother, who was allegedly crazy, during the civil war era. "My grandpa met the woman and ended up buying the house when my father was a little boy," she says. ○

*Photographs by Mònica Bedmar & Translation by Adriana Jaime*

# THE BEACH HOUSE

*Manly, Sydney, Australia*

**RESIDENTS** Jessie and Russ James

**OCCUPATIONS** Jessie: paper goods shop owner. Russ: general manager

**TYPE OF HOUSE** Brick and sandstone apartment

**YEAR BUILT** 1910

"I would say simple, but most people would probably say white," is the way Jessie describes the bright, light, federation-style apartment she lives in with her husband, Russ, on the top floor of what was once a grand old house in New South Wales. Their brick and sandstone flat is covered by rambling ivy and vines and situated on a hill that overlooks the beach on one side and the harbor on the other. It borders on a small but wild native bushland with stone steps leading down to the water. Their neighborhood is centered on the beach, and much of their time is spent walking to and from the ocean or to the nearby national park, often passing their neighbors along the way. The previous owner of their home had lived

there for more than 20 years and left the place quite run-down. "There was even a stack of phone books left behind that reached up past the door frame, one for each of the past 20 years!" she says. "Before we moved in, we stripped out three layers of very old carpet, peeled off velvet wallpaper, removed black vinyl from the bathroom and scrubbed the smoke-stained walls." It was tricky getting some of their things and building materials up the narrow stairs that bend in the middle, forcing them to hoist a couch up through a window at one point. Now that the renovations have been completed, people often remark that being there feels like a holiday (having a beach view certainly doesn't hurt). The couple spends most of

their time in their long, galley-style kitchen that they built from the ground up: They designed it with function in mind so they could spend all their time cooking meals and trying new things. When it comes to decor, they like to keep things simple, choosing to keep everyday objects that are well-made and functional and collecting only things that are useful or meaningful. "Because of that, we have quite a minimal home filled only with things that are well-used and loved," she says. "We also love collecting items found in nature or things with a past that have come from relatives, flea markets or the side of the road." ○

*Photographs by Luisa Brimble*

# THE PALE PALACE

*Wiesbaden, Germany*

**RESIDENTS** Lea Korzeczek and Matthias Hiller
**OCCUPATIONS** Creative directors and founders of design firm Studio Oink
**TYPE OF HOUSE** Old apartment building
**YEAR BUILT** 1900

When Lea and Matthias moved into a 114-year-old Wilhelminian-style building, they had their work cut out for them. "We felt there was beauty hiding behind the dilapidated surface," Lea says. "But we love cracks and traces of former times, so this was the ideal place for us." Their elderly landlord, who prefers PVC to hardwood floors as it's easier to clean, was suspicious of their plans. But the couple was happy to put in the hard work to create a comfortable home. Located in a neighborhood full of young families and hippies in the popular winemaking region of Wiesbaden, the interior was created specifically for and by them. "We love the simple textures of Scandinavian homes and even the *grandezza* of the Italian way of life,"

Lea says. Nearly all the fixtures in their home have been handmade, including a pedestal bed. The space has a facade that reminds them of a cloud. The kitchen centerpiece is a cupboard made of antique windows and the eating space was designed to accommodate their love of cooking, where they make fresh meals at home every day. "We try to get everything from our region and our courtyard garden," she says. "It's important for us to know what we eat." Lea believes that decorating should come from your heart: "Throw away everything you don't need in your daily life except personal things." ○

*Photographs by Studio Oink*

# THE URBAN JUNGLE
*Slipi, Jakarta, Indonesia*

**RESIDENTS** Karin Wijaya and family
**OCCUPATION** Stylist
**TYPE OF HOUSE** Spanish colonial architecture
**YEAR BUILT** Circa 1970

In a humid paradise where the sun shines nearly every day of the year, there doesn't need to be a boundary between house and garden. Jakarta's lack of public parks meant that Karin's family decided to build a natural sanctuary within their own abode. Using half of their land, they planted mango, guava and palm trees, chili plants, aloe vera bushes and a huge herb patch, turning their surroundings into a mini tropical forest. The jungle sprawls into the home where Karin and her mother, sister, brother-in-law and cute two-year-old niece live. They cram plants in every possible space: orchids and anthurium, heliconia and banana leaves. "There's no such thing as too many plants. They're the most important furniture for me," Karin says. Her home does contain non-floral material though, reflecting her respect for the different cultures, religions and colors of the world. In a single room, a Chinese porcelain vase stands in front of a psychedelic painting from India, a Botero print hangs above an Indonesian tribal mask, and framed Yoshitomo Nara postcards and a Danish-style ghost chair sit next to each other, a "compilation album" of her interests. Many years ago when her father, a jazz pianist, was still alive, the house was filled with a different kind of music, but now Karin is making some visual harmonies of her own. ○

*Photographs by Vicky Tanzil*

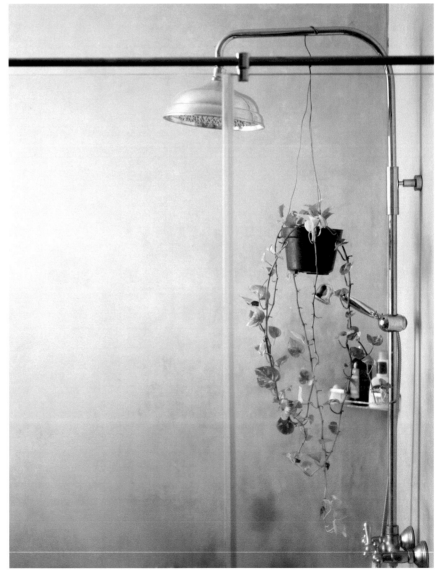

# THE SPANISH VILLA

*Gondomar, Galicia, Spain*

**RESIDENTS** Mònica Bedmar, Álvaro Sanz and from time to time Nanook, Álvaro's son

**OCCUPATIONS** Mònica: photographer and art director. Álvaro: film director and photographer

**TYPE OF HOUSE** Traditional Galician-style granite stone house

**YEAR BUILT** 19th century

---

"The first time we saw it, we knew we wanted to live in it," Mònica says about her austere, rustic home in northwestern Spain. "The bright *galería*, the area and its proximity to the sea were the main factors for us." A traditional Galician structure made of stone, the house still features many of the original fixtures. Many Galician houses used to have *galerías* (a glass-paneled balcony), but most have been replaced in modern times with walls or windows. "It's a total treat that this one was kept: It provides beautiful light all day long and you can see the sea and the sunset," she says. The couple works at home, so they spend a lot of time in their glass office. Their routine changes with the seasons, spending time relaxing in the garden during the summer and reading indoors in the winter. Although it took them a while to feel settled, they now feel at home there. "We used to live in a house in the Galician inland, but it was very cold. This house has helped us find a balance between nature and civilization. It has a powerful energy and we feel protected by it," she says. It's been a refuge for the couple, and they love having people over. "We take walks and bring back small treasures that we use to decorate the house, filling it with memories. We can hear horses going by all the time and you always bump into cows or sheep in the street." ○

*Photographs by Mònica Bedmar & Translation by Lupe Núñez-Fernández*

SPECIAL THANKS
*Paintings* Katie Stratton

Partnership with Kodak

# Kodak alaris

ON THE COVER
*Photograph by* Maia Flore

LIVING FOR ONE, TWO AND A FEW ESSAYS
*Ceramist* Frances Palmer
*Shoes by* Marcella Kurowski

BECOMING YOUR HOME
Thanks to the Hotel Langlois in Paris
*Stylist* Joy Dreyfus

HOME AWAY FROM HOME
*Photograph courtesy of* Wythe Hotel

DREAMING IN CARDBOARD
*Set Designer* Helen MacIntyre
*Stylist* Rachel Caulfield at Era Management London
*Hair & Makeup* Hester at Era Management
London using Aveda
*Models* Indigo, Jahmari and Willow at Kids London
Emily Mae at Grace and Galor

CLOTHING
*Emily Mae wears* sweater by Bonpoint; floral dress by
Marmalade and Mash; and sandals by Massimo Dutti.

*Indigo wears* blue Olympic shirt by Bobo Choses; pale
blue shorts by Bonpoint; and loafers by Step 2wo.

*Willow wears* mustard-colored top and striped
yellow skirt by Caramel Baby and Child; and slip-on
shoes by Stella McCartney.

*Jahmari wears* top by American Apparel; jacket by Stella
McCartney; sweatpants by GRO; and shoes by Bonpoint.

CALIFORNIA DREAMING
*Styling & Props* Lisa Moir
*Food Stylist* Val Aikman-Smith

THE CONCEPT OF HOME
*Thanks to the writers who contributed:*
Louisa Thomsen Brits
Shelby Gill
Jordan Hernandez
Rebecca Parker Payne
Mike Perry
Austin Sailsbury
Molly Yeh

THE CHEF'S KITCHEN: RECIPES
*Food Stylist* Camille Becerra
Thanks to Kitty Cooper and Sophie Orbaum

HOME TOURS OPENER
*Map from the Library of Congress*: Historic American
Buildings Survey/Historic American Engineering
Record/Historic American Landscapes Survey,
Prints & Photographs Division, Library of
Congress, HABS MASS, 9-CAMB, 26--8

THE SELF-MADE MODERNIST
*Translation* Tina Minami Dhingra

THE CLASSIC SEVEN
*Prop Stylist* Pam Morris

THE NATURAL TRADITION
*Translation* Sakiko Setaka
Thanks to Yukiko Kuroda (kurodayukiko.com)

THE FAMILY HEIRLOOM
*Translation & Stylist* Nathalie Schwer

THE HATCH HOUSE
Thanks to Peter McMahon

THE MOUNTAIN CABIN
Thanks to Neus Casanova
*Translation* Adriana Jaime

THE SPANISH VILLA
*Translation* Lupe Núñez-Fernández
*Photography assistance* Álvaro Sanz

ENDNOTES

THE HATCH HOUSE
We used information with permission from *Cape Cod
Modern: Midcentury Architecture and Community on
the Outer Cape* (working title), by Peter McMahon and
Christine Cipriani, published by DAP / Metropolis
Books, released spring 2014.

# SUBSCRIBE

VISIT WWW.KINFOLK.COM/SHOP

FOUR ISSUES EACH YEAR

---

### CONTACT US

If you have questions or comments,
contact us at *info@kinfolk.com*

### SUBSCRIPTIONS

For questions about your subscription,
email us at *subscribe@kinfolk.com*

### STOCKISTS

If you'd like to carry *Kinfolk*,
get in touch at *distribution@kinfolk.com*

### SUBMISSIONS

To pitch a story, write us at
*submissions@kinfolk.com*

WWW.KINFOLK.COM

WWW.KINFOLK.COM

# KEEP IN TOUCH